THE LIBRARY

COLBY JUNIOR COLLEGE

Self-Portrait. Charcoal, 12 x 9. 1908.

514-080

MARSDEN HARTLEY

Elizabeth McCausland

UNIVERSITY OF MINNESOTA PRESS · MINNEAPOLIS

LONDON · GEOFFREY CUMBERLEGE · OXFORD UNIVERSITY PRESS

*ND
237
H3435
M3*

Copyright 1952 by the
UNIVERSITY OF MINNESOTA

All rights reserved. No part of this book
may be reproduced in any form without
the written permission of the publisher.
Permission is hereby granted to review-
ers to quote brief passages in a review to
be printed in a magazine or newspaper.

PRINTED AT THE NORTH CENTRAL PUBLISHING COMPANY, ST. PAUL

LIBRARY OF CONGRESS CATALOG CARD NUMBER: 52–7483

36295

Und so lang du das nicht hast,
dieses Stirb und Werde!
Bist du nur ein trüber Gast
auf der dunkeln Erde.

GOETHE

FOREWORD

THIS monograph on Marsden Hartley, written by Elizabeth McCausland, is the first of a number of volumes on contemporary American artists projected by the University of Minnesota. The utter neglect of American art by American art historians and critics that has persisted until very recently is one of the more curious phenomena in the history of art research. The appearance of the general histories of painting by Larkin and Barker and the survey of modern American painting by Baur filled a gap that was probably unique to the United States. Although the last ten years have seen a most remarkable upsurge of writing on American art there are still very few sound studies of our major artists. There are, in fact, very few serious historians and critics who have published extensively on American painting and sculpture. To the names mentioned one would obviously add Lloyd Goodrich and remember the important contributions of Holger Cahill, William Sawitzky, and E. P. Richardson. One would recall a few significant catalogues, and individuals from whom a contribution may some day be expected. And, aside from Elizabeth McCausland, that is almost the entire story.

In any list of critics of American art the name of Miss McCausland must occupy a high and in some ways a unique place. Working much of the time as an independent research scholar, she has devoted her entire life to the study of American art. Although her long association with the *Springfield Republican* as art critic led her into the examination of many national styles, although she has published works on Picasso and Käthe Kollwitz among others, her major research and publication has been in the field of American painting. Her volumes on Alfred Maurer, George Inness, Edward Lamson Henry, Charles W. Hawthorne, and American subject painting, as well as her innumerable articles and reviews on all phases of American art, constitute a major contribution. Her monograph *American Processional*, produced on the occasion of the Corcoran Gallery exhibition, is actually, as Oliver Larkin pointed out, "A brilliant short history of the American people" seen through artists' eyes.

The monograph on Hartley which Miss McCausland has developed on the base of a catalogue of the Hartleys in the Mr. and Mrs. Hudson D. Walker Collection (now on long-term loan to the University Gallery, University of Minnesota) is the first detailed study of one of our most significant and interesting twentieth-century painters, one who with Maurer and a few others best illustrates the range of complex interrelationships, influences, and conflicts between the modern movements in Europe and America. The monograph gives us an extensive and illuminating critical evaluation, a biographical essay, an extensive bibliography, and the basis for a chronology of Hartley's stylistic development. It is a work that not only establishes the groundwork for all future research on Hartley but also suggests innumerable problems concerning modern American art which need further exploration.

H. HARVARD ARNASON

ACKNOWLEDGMENTS

THANKS for cooperation on this brief introduction to the life and work of
Marsden Hartley are due many individuals though only a few are noted
here. The basic core of research for the monograph is the archive assembled
by the American Art Research Council, for the most part in 1944 and 1945,
assisted by Hudson D. Walker, and generously made available to me. That
record was compiled by Rosalind Irvine, secretary of the council and assistant curator of the Whitney Museum of American Art, with the advice
of Lloyd Goodrich, director of the council and associate director of the
Whitney Museum, and with the cooperation of museums and private col-
lectors, as well as of friends of the artist. All these will have to be given
blanket thanks at this time and wait for personal acknowledgments when
my critical biography of Hartley is published. Since this file was assembled,
much new material has come to light and been added to the archive. This
record, however, has enabled me to save a considerable amount of time
and will be even more valuable for the long-range study.

As in the case of A. H. Maurer, Hudson Walker has been an enthusiastic
and devoted supporter of the proposition that American artists should be
thoroughly recorded and studied, to the end that fundamental American art
literature may comprise the major figures in our native tradition. If he, as
a New York art dealer in the 1930s, had not believed in Hartley as a painter
and given him material and moral support, there might have been far less
to write about Hartley's creative achievement; for it was in the last years
of his life that Hartley flowered, thanks (I firmly believe) to the encourage-
ment and opportunity then given him, in which Hudson Walker was a

germinal influence. Further, as ancillary executor of the Hartley estate, Hudson Walker was able to give assistance to the American Art Research Council's survey, which immensely facilitated that work. Again, as with my Maurer study, thanks are due Ione Gaul Walker, whose studio was invaded so that the Hartleys in the Walkers' Forest Hills home could be photographed and studied.

My warmest thanks go to those members of the staff of the University of Minnesota who made it possible for me to study the Hartleys on long-term loan there — even amid blizzards and ten-foot snowdrifts. The University Gallery's director, Mrs. J. C. Lawrence, extended many courtesies and facilities and showed a lively interest in the Hartley exhibition and book. Betty Maurstad, museum assistant, was of the greatest aid in checking the paintings and prints and in coordinating the gallery's records with my own. Carl Hawkinson and his department did an essential task in transporting almost one hundred works from storage to suitable workrooms; and Lyle Rowe helped substantially in the physically laborious work of shifting paintings, holding them up for examination, and the like, as well as taking down color notes from dictation. Patricia Peeke, of the University Library, was cooperative and helpful, as was Jean Huddleston of the University Gallery. Harvey Retzloff is to be thanked for the photographs of the Hartleys which were studied at the gallery in March 1951. Other gallery staff members will, again, have to get blanket thanks.

Research was divided because not all the works in the Walker Collection had been shipped to Minneapolis at the time of my field trip. Some, as said above, were seen at the Walkers' home. Others were seen at various dealers, notably the Paul Rosenberg Gallery; and Florence Walters deserves thanks for her cooperation. A collateral aspect of the study was to examine Hartleys from the Alfred Stieglitz Collection which had passed into the possession of E. Weyhe; and thanks are due Martha L. Dickinson of that gallery for her generous assistance in allowing me to see these in storage. W. Joseph Fulton very kindly lent me microfilm material on some of Hartley's correspondence.

As always the New York Public Library and the Frick Art Reference Library have rendered generous cooperation, and the Cooper Union Library staff is to be thanked for technical assistance. Other special services are those of Oliver Baker of New York, who photographed most of the Hartleys there, and of Mrs. Ingrid-Märta Held, staff restorer of the New-York Historical Society, who cleaned and relined various works in New York and obtained for us comparison photographs after cleaning, as well as also working on some of the Hartleys at the University Gallery. Berenice Abbott helped out with an unavoidable last-minute rush of filing and collating photographs; and Mrs. Julia J. Schneer found time in her free hours from regular employment to work on the rush job of typing.

All those who helped deserve warmer thanks than the printed word.

E. McC.

CONTENTS

ILLUSTRATIONS

The crayon drawing of Dead Plover, 1940, *has been
cropped for use on the front cover*

MARSDEN HARTLEY

MARSDEN HARTLEY

MARSDEN HARTLEY'S LIFE made a full circle before its close. At the end the "Maine-iac" — as he called himself — came home to Maine: he had been born January 4, 1877, at Lewiston, and he died September 2, 1943, at Ellsworth. Before his life closed, he passed through the intricacies of post-impressionism, cubism, fauvism, symbolism, and expressionism, only to return to realism, as he returned to his native land. For most of his working years he renounced subject matter–content and asserted that the painting is all, and all-sufficing. Only at the end of his life, when he had long been driven by ill health and economic anxieties, did he come back to nature. He had scorned the lonely, desolate land of his birth. In it at last he found not only peace and human company but the fulfillment of his need to be himself. In the companionship of drowned fishermen, eroded shells, sea birds dead on the beach after the hurricane, he found that sense of persisting and meaningful life he had not found in art coteries and salons. Still a lonely man, he was less lonely because he learned to share the loneliness of the elements. So he grew to know the meaning of the sea's incessant beating on rock and sand, of strong-winged gulls breasting the storm, of simple fisherfolk whose daily round encompassed the death of their beloved sons. Fleeing from the Maine hillsides and valleys he had known as a boy and a youth, returning to the Maine rivers, bays, and mountains he knew as an aging, discouraged, ailing man, Hartley completed the circle of his life. He had written his own epitaph long before, in 1918, in a poem, "After Battle":

> . . . And let them have the sea
> Who want eternity.

Marsden Hartley was the youngest child of Thomas and Mary (Horbury) Hartley, the only boy in a family of nine children. Christened Edmund, he took his adopted name from his stepmother's maiden name. One painting has been located which is signed *Edmund Marsden Hartley*. This is *Storm Clouds, Maine*, dated here 1908, though it may have been painted earlier. Thereafter he signed himself, when he signed at all, *Marsden Hartley*. The change of name is interesting, revealing as it does his deep attachment to his father's second wife.

Records of Hartley's childhood are sparse, unless as yet undiscovered or undeclared papers come to light. He was always interested in intellectual pursuits, reading omnivorously all his life, as he wrote copiously all his life. At thirteen he made drawings of moths, butterflies, and flowers for a local naturalist. Thus early he committed himself to art. When the family moved to Cleveland, he studied with John Semon and then, winning a scholarship at the Cleveland School of Art, with Cullen Yates and Nina Waldeck. He seems also to have attended a sketch class conducted by a Miss Caroline Sowers in her home where a half-dozen youths "were endeavoring to . . . get an education without benefit of college."

Even at that time he was searching for masters from whom to take instruction. He once told an art school associate that he had gone to call on George Inness, whose work he admired. This must have been in 1894 or earlier, since Inness died in that year, and Hartley would then have been sixteen or seventeen. His search for masters persisted in the 1900s. Besides the Segantini influence remarked by critics on the occasion of his first exhibition, he was deeply influenced by Ryder, an influence which recurred at different times in his painting. There walks through the pages of Hartley's letters and other writings the shadowy figure of the aged and fabulous Albert Pinkham Ryder, seen on Fifteenth Street in New York, at the bakery which the young Alfred Kreymborg and Alanson Hartpence frequented, sometimes with Hartley. Ryder, wrote Hartley, walked only by night, and Hartley had lived on the same street for eight or nine years before he met

Ryder. Hartley's portrait of Ryder, painted thirty years later, is a masterpiece of American folklore: few artists have used other artists as their heroes.

Coming to New York in 1898, Hartley studied at the Chase school with F. Luis Mora, the late Frank Vincent Du Mond, and William Merritt Chase himself. By 1900 he was disillusioned with what he described as the superficiality of the Chase system and decided to attend classes at the National Academy of Design. There, he wrote a friend, he would study life with George Maynard and composition with Edwin H. Blashfield. Apparently, according to other sources, he also studied there with F. J. Dillman and Edgar Ward, the latter a teacher of A. H. Maurer in the 1890s. The Academy classes had, Hartley felt, the advantage of being conducted in an orderly way. He needed, he thought, more elementary work and so would study antique and life. Later he wrote that he liked the Academy exceedingly well, and especially the instructor in antique.

This bit of autobiography is interesting because one of Hartley's school friends criticized his "drawing from the life," and his work itself seems to suggest that he never mastered academic draftsmanship completely. For example, the massive volumes of some of his late drawings of the male and female nude seem clumsy rather than purposive, as do the hands, for example, of his portraits of fishermen. At this time Hartley, in addition, was attending the artist's-artisan's school on East Thirty-third Street.

In the summer of 1900 he returned to Lewiston to paint. It seemed strange, he wrote, to be in such a small place after seven years in a large city. In the summer of 1901 he planned exuberantly to leave Lewiston to spend the season with "artist socialists" at North Bridgton. He looked forward to meeting George de Forest Brush, who had a summer place nearby, and also Douglas Volk, who would be in the vicinity of the village of Sweden. Thereafter, for almost a decade, Hartley lived in Maine during the summers and in New York during the winters. For a time N. E. Montross made him a weekly grant of four dollars. Hartley fought his battle privately for the most part, and scant record of his first thirty years survives. Twenty years

5

later Hartley was to write of Maine as if it were too painful to be remembered.

Hartley was thirty-two when he found a champion. In May 1909, Alfred Stieglitz, who had exhibited Maurer and John Marin in April, gave Hartley a one-man exhibition in the Photo-Secession Gallery at 291 Fifth Avenue. Stieglitz documented the event in *Camera Work* with the statement that here was "a new painter whose efforts to express himself in a personal way deserved that he be given an opportunity to reach the public." The note added: "His technique is unusual and his interpretation of sky, mountain and woods in brilliant coloring is of a decorative rather than realistic effect."

Writing in a later issue, the critic Charles H. Caffin analyzed "Unphotographic Paint: — The Texture of Impressionism," as follows. Hartley's "small collection" of oils "were examples of an extreme and up-to-date impressionism. They represented winter scenes agitated by snow and wind, 'proud music of the storm'; wood interiors, strange entanglements of tree-trunks; and mountain slopes covered with autumn woods with some island-dotted river winding along their base." The critic added: "Hartley's technique is interesting though not necessarily original. It is a version of the famous Segantini 'stitch,' of using colors pure and simple and laying them side by side upon the canvas in long flecks that look like stitches of embroidery."

Till World War I closed 291, Stieglitz exhibited Hartley's work, as he did intermittently in the 1920s and the 1930s. In 1910 he showed a group of "Younger American Painters," comprising Brinley, Carles, Dove, Fellowes, Hartley, Marin, Maurer, Steichen, and Max Weber. In 1912, 1914, 1916, and 1917, he gave Hartley one-man shows; and it was Stieglitz with Arthur B. Davies who in 1912 helped raise money so that Hartley was able to go abroad for the first time, at the age of thirty-five, and so to experience at first hand the excitements and enthusiasms of modern art, which many other American painters and sculptors had been assimilating for some years, Maurer since 1897.

Thenceforth Hartley would spend much time abroad and in travel. He was in Paris and Berlin in 1912 and 1913, and he returned to Europe in the

Storm Clouds, Maine. Oil, 30½ x 25½. 1908.

Landscape No. 29. Oil, 9⅜ x 5¼. 1907?

Autumn. Oil, 30 x 30. 1908.

spring of 1914 after a brief visit to the United States at the end of 1913. Coming back from war-torn Europe at the end of 1915, Hartley visited Bermuda and Provincetown in 1916. At Provincetown he spent the summer as the guest of John Reed and shared in the ferment of intellectual vanguardism then beginning there. In an unpublished manuscript, "The Spangle of Existence," he writes of Mary Heaton Vorse, Neith and Hutchins Hapgood, Louise Bryant, Carl Sprinchorn, and that mythical Greenwich Village character, the anarchist Hippolyte Havel, who at that time was acting as cook for Reed.

In 1917 he went back to Maine. About this time he became interested in the American folk art of painting on glass, an art which he compared with the popular art of painting decorations on saloon windows. In 1918, with a grant from the veteran art dealer Charles L. Daniel, Hartley went to Taos, New Mexico, where he worked for two years, with side trips to Santa Fe and California. He never returned to the Southwest though ten and fifteen years later he wrote of his desire to do so. Somehow disillusionment had overtaken him, and he wrote in the 1930s that Taos should be spelled "chaos."

Again, in 1921, he was assisted to go abroad. Stieglitz and Mitchell Kennerly organized an auction of the work in his studio, and 117 oils, pastels, and paintings on glass brought a total of about five thousand dollars. Some of the Hartleys in the present collection were in the 1921 sale, as may be read from the numbers penciled in blue chalk or crayon on the backs of the pictures.

Hartley remained abroad, living variously in Paris, Berlin, and the south of France, till the world economic crisis of 1929 forced his return, along with many so-called expatriates. In these years, though his income from sales was not great, he found patrons who underwrote his work, among them William C. Bullitt. He made trips to the United States, in 1924 and again in 1928. In 1924 he settled in Vence in the Maritime Alps and painted there for two years. By 1926 he had moved to Aix-en-Provence, vowing to take up where Cézanne had left off. In 1927, he did not paint at all but

8

worked at drawing, especially with silver point. He loved this delicate medium but found it hard on his eyes, a fact which he lamented, as he did the fact that pastels are difficult to care for and to transport.

After his return to the United States, Hartley searched for roots. He spent the summer of 1930 at Franconia Notch, a terrain which proved to be morally painful and enervating. In 1931 he found new creative energy among the glacial remains of the moraine of Gloucester's Dogtown Common. In the spring of this year he had been awarded a Guggenheim fellowship, but he did not use it till the following year when he went to Mexico. Again he did not find the congenial spiritual climate he was seeking. Yet Popocatepetl fascinated him, and he painted the volcano in many symbolic guises, perfecting a triangular compositional form which would finally come into its own in the Mt. Katahdins painted toward the end of his life. One fine canvas came from this period, Hartley's memorial to the poet Hart Crane, *Eight Bells' Folly*, which foreshadows the seascapes of 1936. From Mexico he fled in disillusionment once more, this time to Germany, where he painted his Garmisch-Partenkirchen series during the winter of 1933/1934.

Thenceforth the tempo of his production accelerated. Hartley returned to the United States to paint Dogtown again, in the summer of 1934. In 1935 he painted Bermuda sea flora in semitropic fantasies, as he called his "sky-blue-pink fish." Later that season he found his way to Nova Scotia to paint the sturdy fishing folk there. In 1936 he was once more engrossed with Dogtown, though now in a storm-tossed and frantic spirit, as he remembered *The Last of the Stone Wall*. In this year, too, Nova Scotia held his attention. In 1937 he began to paint Georgetown, Maine, landscapes. In the next year he would paint the remarkable series he called "archaic portraits," of the Nova Scotian family whose two sons were drowned at sea, and with these the first version of *Fishermen's Last Supper*, his preliminary cartoon for a mural planned for a fishermen's bethel (or chapel) which was never built.

In 1937/1938 and in 1938/1939 he painted the group of Vinalhaven landscapes which include the richest and most darkly luminous of his Maine subjects, among them *Waterfall, Morse Pond*; *Camden Hills from Baker's Island*; and *Robin Hood Cove.* The self-styled "Maine-iac" had come back to Maine, determined to be the best painter of the subject matter of Maine, as he was (he said) the only artist painting Maine who was a native-born son.

Through these years there was threaded a constant interest in the flora and fauna he had begun to draw at thirteen. He painted garden flowers and bouquets of roses, the delightful forms and shapes of squid, lobster, crab, and bream, and (tragically) roses for gulls that lost their way at sea. In his still life he found room for ladies' gloves and for white cotton work gloves, for odds and ends of spliced rope, and for shells worn by the tides. He saw fishing fleets set off for the Great Banks and he saw coastwise storms beat on the base of the lighthouse. In the forests of Maine he saw the ghosts of forest fires and denuded timberlands, but he saw also the abundant harvest of logs floated down the rivers. In autumn and in winter he saw Mt. Katahdin raise its peak above the Maine mountainside, not as lofty as Popocatepetl but nonetheless majestic.

In the last years of his life Hartley remembered Ryder as he had seen him long before walking the New York streets at night. He thought of an American hero like Lincoln and painted him as the beardless *Young Worshipper of the Truth* and as a *Great Good Man*, bearded. The waves dashed high, and the winter grew inclement. Gulls and plover lay dead on the beach. Roses were their memorial. Thinking of the chaos of war, Hartley found a new interest in religious symbolism, as in his young manhood he had professed religious convictions. He turned to the literature of mysticism for themes, as in his paintings of John Donne and Richard Rolle of Hampole. He took a classical motif of Christian art to make a powerful expressionist painting, *Three Friends*. He made other paintings of Christ surrounded by half-naked men and of subjects which echo the deposition from the cross and the entombment, and of a beggar praying on Park Avenue. Finally he painted that last sheaf of *Roses* as if in acute foreknowl-

Carnival of Autumn. Oil, 30 x 30. 1908.

Maine Snowstorm. Oil, 30 x 30. 1908.

edge of approaching death. The canvas was on his easel when he died. So his life ended at the age of sixty-six. He had painted perhaps a thousand pictures and written four books and many articles, as well as unpublished matter. In spite of difficulties and discouragements, Hartley had managed to have his say. What was it he said?

II

Hartley would have answered, at the beginning of his student's life in New York at the turn of the century, that he wished to speak of communion with beloved nature. Nature had, he wrote, a balm for every pain. He believed that beauty was the artist's one aim. To express nature divine and to glorify the god who provides such beauties, to speak truth in all things, was the artist's mission, he stated, and he did not look upon technical achievement as art. Communing with birds and butterflies and making color notes of brilliant nature, the young artist brooded on the artist's role.

Yet in his first public appearance a decade later at 291, he was represented by paintings which seem the negation of nature. The many small oils of 1908 (painted for the most part on wood or academy board panels variously 9 x 12, 12 x 12, and 12 x 14) show a sharp break with his *Landscape No. 29* (1907?). Woods and hills in summer, in autumn, and in winter are represented in an advanced impressionist manner, probably a more radi-

12

Landscape No. 36.
Oil, 30 x 34. 1909.

cal use of this technic than any other Americans were then employing. The small-sized panels did not allow Hartley scope for the elaborate impasto of his 30 x 30 oils, *Carnival of Autumn, Autumn,* and *Maine Snowstorm,* all painted before May 1909. But they show by what steps Hartley broke with the Academy and the dwindling American tradition of naturalism, to become one of the pioneers of modern art in America.

As Charles Caffin had pointed out in what must be the first critique of Hartley's work, in *Camera Work,* the "unphotographic" character of paint used in the impressionist manner denies the function of naturalist painting, which is the rendering of a literal scientific transcript of nature. The artist's attention in impressionist painting became centered on the surface of the painting, as impressionist theory sought to reproduce atmosphere and light through color divided according to an incorrect optical definition. When Hartley was won over to the Segantini "stitch," he must have known this self-taught protoimpressionist only through reproductions in magazines and art books. Even today, it seems that there are few paintings by Segantini owned in the United States.

From studying reproductions, of which many may be found in the art

13

magazines of the 1900s, Hartley must have learned how Segantini's paint texture carried on the researches of French impressionism. In his painting before May 1909, he made great play with the style. In fact, in *Autumn* the stitch is so exaggerated that the impasto is often one eighth of an inch deep, and more. This is true, also, of *Carnival of Autumn*, which may be identified by Caffin's reference to an "island-dotted river."

As Hartley had written in 1900, he was not concerned primarily with drawing but with color. This concern continued throughout his life; and surely he is one of the finest of contemporary American colorists, especially in his last work, in which deep color usurps the role of deep space. One may add that in his later critical writings on problems of art and on his own aesthetic convictions, Hartley dismissed Segantini as but one of the influences in his creative development. Yet it is clear by internal evidence that Hartley owed to Segantini a strong incentive to break with American naturalism.

This is demonstrated also in Hartley's long-standing interest in letters. Early in the century he made the acquaintance of Wallace Gould, the imagist poet, in Maine; and in the second decade of the century he pleaded Gould's cause with Harriet Monroe, editor of the vanguard magazine *Poetry*. Nurtured on Emerson, Francis Thompson, and Emily Dickinson, Hartley must have found the revolt of imagism as enthralling as the revolt of impressionism. Written in Hartley's hand on the back of the 11 7/8 x 8 7/8 panel *Landscape No. 16*, 1908, is a poem, which has been partially obliterated. It reads:

OCTOBER DYING

October Lies (?) — Dying
The dead dance frantically!
Before my eyes —
shivering ghosts of immemorial°
all there is is waste of
long forgotten beauty.
Dead — dead — they dance!
Frantically —

° *Glorious* is crossed out here and *immemorial* written above.

14

Deserted Farm. Oil, 24 x 20. 1909.

Glad for the last wild dance
[The next line is illegible.]
With bits of gold & ruby
Dangling from their [rest illegible]
But they dance! dance! dance!
Frantically, divinely
Against the Turquoise.

This was no accidental or casual bit of automatic writing; for another small panel, *Landscape No. 15*, 1908, now in the collection of E. Weyhe, is inscribed on the back with another example of Hartley's early *vers libre*. The two small works were in the collection of Alfred Stieglitz until that was dispersed in 1949, so that the connection is obvious. The second poem reads:

In the Beau Shop
The blithering drooling idiots
Sit — sit — sit
Lolling and sprawling
In the green gloom of a
soot smeared lamp —
Sitting and sitting
falling and crawling
over each other
Drooling in the spit box! —
And they sit and sprawl
Fall & crawl
In and out
of the grey green gloom!
Blithering idiots all —

The disillusionment of the second poem clearly must be related to the phase of melancholy which led to Hartley's "dark mountain" period, as Stieglitz used to refer to paintings like *Deserted Farm*, 1909. Content aside, Hartley was breaking up the old shapes of language as he sought to break up the shapes of nature. In the end he came back to nature, but with a new vision.

With the moral and material support of Stieglitz and of N. E. Montross and Charles L. Daniel and finally of Hudson D. Walker, Hartley was enabled to carry on his aesthetic search for thirty years. In essence he may be said to be a mirror of our age, an age of aesthetic eclecticism and fragmentation. And he may be called a man of his time precisely because he shows forth in his life and work the period's intellectual conflicts. Fragmented by schools, confused by the lack of a common language, artists today seek to define their use in society. Now, in spite of the academy of abstractionism, a half-century's denial of subject matter and communication as functions of art is being subjected to re-examination. Hartley anticipated the challenge and met the challenge.

The history of his experimentation may be written in terms of the influences to which he reacted. Rarely did he admit that he had been influenced.

Landscape No. 32.
Water color, 14⅛ x 10. 1911.

Still Life No. 12. Oil, 20 x 16. 1910.

Pears. Oil, 16 x 12¼. 1911.

Still Life: Fruit. Oil, 20 x 20¼. 1911.

Abstraction. Oil, 16¼ x 13¼. 1911.

To Ryder, he gave credit as one "who accentuated [Hartley's] already tor-
tured imagination." But he added the reservation that he had lived the life
of the imagination "at too great an expense." Yet it was Ryder who was
Hartley's next important source; and it is Ryder who pervades not only the
early landscapes of 1909, such as *Deserted Farm,* but also the recollections
of New Mexico Hartley painted in Germany in 1922, such as *Paysage.* The
year 1909 was a difficult one for Hartley, and thoughts of death preoccupied
him, as they did many another time. The bleakness of New England filled
his heart, and for almost thirty years he saw his native land only as blighted,
cold, sterile, and unfriendly to the soul.

Yet other influences were to steal him away from Ryder. At 291, in 1908,
he saw the work of Matisse for the first time. By March 1910, when the
"Younger American Painters" held their group exhibition there, Hartley had
been won over to postimpressionist still life. His "livid cucumber," his
"dreary plantains" (or perhaps they were bananas — critics differed), his
pears, all were painted with dark, heavy outlines. The drawing of his jugs
of "royal blue" was visibly related to the Academy's antique class. But there

Still Life. Oil, 32⅛ x 25⅝. 1912.

had been a change. The perspective began to show a double point of view, the design was becoming flat and linear, and decorative aspects were stressed instead of realism.

In 1910 and 1911 Stieglitz showed work by Cézanne and by Picasso. By a fortunate chance, there survives the first painting Hartley made after he saw examples of Picasso's analytical cubism, exhibited at 291. This is *Landscape No. 32*, painted in 1911. Another surviving early work of Hartley's is *Still Life: Fruit*, 1911, which reflects the influence of Cézanne. By the study of these and by comparison with the Picassos reproduced in *Camera Work* in 1911 and 1912, I have come to the conclusion that the blue *Abstraction* shown in the Museum of Modern Art's 1951 exhibition, "Abstract Painting and Sculpture in America," may also be dated 1911. For it is reasonable to assume that Hartley assimilated the Cézanne and Picasso influences before rather than after he went abroad in 1912. Already by April 1912, *Camera Work* was reprinting J. E. Chamberlin's *New York Mail* criticism which called Hartley "another of our 'fauves'" and "the gentle painter of super-heated still life and rainbow landscapes."

Abstraction with Flowers. Oil, 39½ x 31½. 1913.

Hartley was always, it seems, highly susceptible to influences. So though the first work he painted when he reached Paris was a characteristically fauvist *Still Life* of decorated textiles and ceramics, arrayed with fruit on a tilted table top, he soon was reflecting new aesthetic orientations. Almost at once he came into the orbit of Kandinsky and other members of the Blue Rider group. Fifteen years later Hartley wrote he was happy that he never did slide down the Kandinsky kaleidoscope; but this is a disingenuous remark. Kandinsky's *The Art of Spiritual Harmony* had been published in Germany in 1911; and excerpts from it were reprinted in *Camera Work* in July 1912, so that its formulations were in the aesthetic aura of the Stieglitz group. Kandinsky's intellectual system was concerned with the triangle, the pyramid, and the circle, as well as with professedly mystic combinations of color. These forms and compositional devices appear in the Hartley canvases *Abstraction with Flowers, Movements, Painting No. 1,* and *Painting No. 2,* which have all been dated 1913 for consistency since some are so dated on the back, though probably the split date 1912/1913 would be more exact.

The period of Kandinsky influence resulted in a number of paintings described as "spot movements" (as one of the canvases in the Walker Collection is inscribed on its back), a phrase Kandinsky popularized in *The Art of Spiritual Harmony.* Yet Hartley early made a punning transferral of the term's meaning to music. One painting of his is inscribed on its face, *Bach: Prelude-et-Fugue,* and there are at least three variations on this theme. His mingling of mediums is characteristic. The facility with which Hartley passed back and forth between painting and writing, as well as from one manner to another, no doubt explains a sense of inconsecutiveness felt as one runs rapidly through the photographic archive of his total production in painting. One may add that a similar lack of continuity is felt as one reads any number of his letters. His very articulateness defeated his endeavor to express himself: many times he failed to make his meaning clear by the quantity and variety of what he said.

Kandinsky had written of "The Movement" that it is based on "melodic

Military.
Oil, 39¼ x 39¼. 1913.

compositions" such as may be seen in the Ravenna mosaics of S. Vitale, Cézanne, Hodler, "the old German masters, the Persians, the Japanese, the Russian Icons," and the like. He called his paintings of 1911 to 1913 "improvisations" when he did not coin literary titles such as *Small Pleasures*, a mannerism also found in Hartley, for example, in *One Portrait of One Woman*. The movement of the triangle, Kandinsky argued, is better than the simple movement; for "the whole triangle is moving slowly, almost invisibly forward and upwards." Of the language of form and color, he wrote further: "A yellow triangle, a blue circle, a green square, or a green triangle, a yellow circle, a blue square — all these . . . have different spiritual values." Finally, of the pyramid, he wrote: "Every man who steeps himself in the spiritual possibilities of his art is a valuable helper in the building of the spiritual pyramid which will some day reach to heaven."

In Hartley's paintings of 1912/1913 these formulations may be seen repeated. The *Bach: Prelude-et-Fugue* series makes use of the musical motif. At the same time, motion is also an element. But whereas the search for kinetic subject matter in such a work as Balla's *Walking Dog* is made by superimposing image on image, in Hartley's series the individual paintings have the function of the individual "frames" in the motion picture film. By

22

the montage of remembered afterimages, the desired goal of movement is attained or, at least, suggested.

In Paris before World War I Hartley had not fully assimilated these new ideas. Like Segantini, Kandinsky provided him with a novel language. Twenty years later, in Mexico in 1932 and 1933, Hartley came back to the pyramid as a basic proposition, extolling Popocatepetl as a fundamental form of nature and endowing it with a sexual symbolism not unlike that commented on by the late Paul Rosenfeld, in *Port of New York*, in his criticism of Hartley's New Mexican landscapes. In 1928, in studies of Mont-Sainte-Victoire, Hartley had modified his pyramid, broadening the base and widening the peak's angle. In the Garmisch-Partenkirchen paintings which followed Popocatepetl, he compressed his triangle and accentuated the height of his pyramid. Finally, in the Katahdin series, he fused nature, abstract concept, and the memory of Hiroshige's Fujiyama, prints of which he had admired as a young man and wrote about in later years. The sequence demonstrates how Hartley learned to synthesize experience and experiment in a moving personal expression.

Interested in the symbolist movement in poetry and a contributor to *Poetry* in its pioneer days, Hartley found time at the beginning of his stay in Europe to experiment with symbolism in painting. The *One Portrait of One Woman* in the Walker Collection no doubt can be deciphered after further study. It is by no means a unique example; a similar tendency occurs in the remembered New Mexican *Santos* of 1920. The manner seems to have lost its attraction for Hartley quickly and was put aside in favor of the objects of prewar Berlin, such as *Military*, 1913. Echoes of the manner served as a bridge, however, in the earlier transitional *Forms Abstracted* of 1913. The hand of expressionism is not yet markedly visible in this painting of a German officer mounted, in full regalia.

Hartley had exhibited in the Armory Show in February 1913 while he was still abroad. The Hartleys recorded have not as yet supplied a clue which might lead to the positive identification of the work he exhibited then. On his return to the United States at the end of 1913 he prepared for

23

his third one-man show at 291, exhibiting the Kandinsky-inspired canvases and some of the prewar Berlin impressions. Forewords by Mabel Dodge, Gertrude Stein, and the artist himself were included in the catalogue. Veteran critic Henry McBride of the *New York Sun*, commenting on the figure eights "which appear here and there in some of Mr. Hartley's German experiences," noted that visitors were annoyed by them. He added that there were no policemen in the paintings, but Uhlan dragoons. Further, Mabel Dodge's reference to mountains was to "other paintings . . . which are not at present on view."

His comments, as well as others in the art press, are interesting indices of the cultural climate of the time, as well as valuable brackets for dating the categories of subject matter. *Camera Work* for January 1914 quoted the *New York Mail*'s J. E. Chamberlin as writing that the paintings were large, painted in kaleidoscopic patterns. One painting was described as showing "a small figure of a soldier on a bright red horse, but [with] the greater part of the canvas . . . occupied by squares, circles and patterns, a large figure 8, and things somewhat like military badges, epaulettes, and other martial objects." A canvas which fills the description in all points save that the horse is an Indian red, not a bright red, may be seen in the collection of American literature at the Yale University Library, one of the Hartley items found in the recent gift of Mabel Dodge Luhan. To complete the picture, the Yale collection possesses one of the epaulettes which Hartley was so fond of including in his "Germanic" series, the gift of the Hartley estate. Chamberlin added: "Another curious picture shows four interwoven circles, or bubbles, at the bottom, with a whirl of light-jets, stars, and a general explosive appearance, filling up the rest of the canvas." This last obviously refers to the series of "movements."

Of them the *New York American*'s Caffin wrote enthusiastically: "Among them is a Paris impression. An explosion has occurred; there is a spread of rocket-like rods, bursting at their tops into flaming stars. It is the volcano's preliminary splutter. Then — to preserve my simile — vapors begin to arise. In the freedom of air and light they take on convolutions of pattern

24

Portrait. Oil, 31¾ x 21⅛. 1914/1915.

and brighter and brighter colors; they take shape and suggestions of Kwannons, triune circles and other Catholic or Rosicrucian symbols. . . . Then gradually the hot cone of the volcano releases itself in a flow of molten lava. It hisses around the jagged edge of the crater's lip and forms in a slowly coiling stream. Only here we have to imagine the crater inverted. The lava zigzags and pours upward."

Hartley returned to Germany in 1914 after his exhibition at 291 and remained there till the end of 1915, when he came back to New York. He celebrated the Fourth of July, 1914, in Berlin by writing a tribute, "What Is 291?" to be published in *Camera Work*. On his second visit, again he made use of German military subject matter, but in a personal and expressive style. The forms abstracted from nature, such as *Berlin Abstraction* and *Portrait*, have an inner unity and power. He has assimilated his symbols and set them forth with authority and impressiveness. His palette is stronger and more interesting than the Kandinsky-esque crepuscule, and the paint itself is handled with a more sensitive concern for the sensuous, physical qualities of the material. The strong reds, yellows, blues, greens, and blacks are full of resonance, as would be the great brass military horns he utilized for visual objects in *Military*.

When Hartley exhibited his second "Germanic" series at 291 in 1916 — after he had gotten the new work past the blockade — he disclaimed the charge that such pictures have any more meaning than any other pictures. Fifteen years afterward he wrote, again, that they were pictorial arrangements of things felt and seen. He added that as a rule pictures can have no meaning, that is, no hidden meaning. In 1916 he had written, in "the leaflet which accompanied the exhibition," as follows: "The forms are only those which I have observed casually from day to day. There is no hidden symbolism whatsoever in them; there is no slight intention of that anywhere. Things under observation, just pictures of any day, any hour. I have expressed only what I have seen. They are merely consultations of the eye — in no sense problem; my notion of the purely pictural."

Nonetheless the influence of expressionism was great, and the more so since Hartley exhibited with the Blue Rider group in Munich at the invitation of Franz Marc and in Berlin in the first German autumn salon organized by *Der Sturm*. His attraction to the emblems of militarism is a question to ponder. In 1934 and 1935 he was criticized by old-time friends for visiting Germany after Hitler's rise to power and seemed not to agree with the moral issue they raised. Yet at about the same time he was painting *Junker* officers in Berlin, he was attracted to the Southwest's Indian art, certainly a pacific culture. This early American art had not become the vogue in 1914 and 1915, and it will be interesting therefore to discover what his source was then. As early as 1900 he had written to a New York friend from Maine, praising the American Museum of Natural History's fine collections of butterflies. Could it have been there that he first saw examples of our continent's original art?

As said above, Hartley returned to the United States late in 1915. His 1914/1915 Berlin paintings were delayed in ocean transit, and it was necessary in consequence to postpone his exhibition at 291 from February 1916 to April and May. As a result the paintings he showed in the 1916 Forum Exhibition were the 1913 "movements," as reference to the one reproduced in the exhibition catalogue proves. Previously Hartley had held his first European one-man show in the Berlin home of Max Liebermann in October 1915. Plans for other exhibitions were necessarily abandoned.

Shortly after his return, when he was staying for a time with the etcher Ernest Roth on West Fourteenth Street, Hartley had his portrait painted by Ben Benn, a work now in the Walker Collection. With his self-portrait of 1908, a somewhat feverish drawing with a hatchwork of broken lines, and with an academic portrait of 1900, painted by an old Academy associate, this gives us the earliest memorabilia of Hartley. In this portrait, as in another painted by Benn in 1924, the portraitist caught Hartley's mood of the moment. In the 1915 portrait, the pattern of the Kandinsky formula has become looser, like tentacles of a sea animal, and the realism of Hartley's aquiline nose (of which he seemed to be extremely proud, to judge from many references in his letters) has been transformed into a romanti-

A Bermuda Window in a Semitropic Character. Oil, 31¾ x 26. 1916.

cally powerful shape. Later, in 1924, when Benn painted Hartley in this country while Hartley was making a short trip to the United States, Benn captured by a sort of spiritual osmosis the quality of the hard, chiseled landscapes Hartley was then painting at Vence.

By 1916, when Hartley was re-established in this country and working variously in Bermuda and Provincetown, he used the word *movement* to describe paintings "abstracted" from the observed visual appearances of nature; a number of the subjects of 1916 and 1917 are clearly derived from sailboats and other marine materials. Symbolism appears again in the incorporation of the names *Elsa* and *Elsa Kobenhavn* into two abstract panels. Somewhat later he applied the term *movements* to still life. All these were painted in flat patterns in arbitrary color. How close Hartley was to the American synchromist movement is a question. Arthur Dove, another early member of the Stieglitz group, at one time was attracted to the theories of synchromism, and Hartley may have been also. Or, again, he may have been influenced by the flat, rectangular cubist design Picasso worked in from 1916 to 1920. If this premise is true, Hartley later denied his source; his correspondence contains extremely unflattering references to Picasso.

28

Movement No. 9. Oil, 24⅛ x 20⅛. 1916.

It is difficult to find documentation to fit *A Bermuda Window* into the sequence of his evolution. The 1921 sale catalogue dates his Bermuda subjects as 1916. According to Hartley's correspondence, he could scarcely have been in Bermuda in 1918. Yet there is a related painting, *Atlantic Window in the New England Character*, dated 1919 in the same catalogue, of which Paul Rosenfeld has given a description which could well apply to the Bermuda scene. In his essay "Marsden Hartley" in *Port of New York*, Rosenfeld wrote: "This regal lily with its wickedly horned leaves, erect between butter-yellow draperies, is felt as a volume against that lustrous purplish-blue sweep of bay, as that is felt against the curve of sandy shore, and the shore in turn felt against the rim of violet peaks and they against the white-clouded summer sky."

Hartley's use of the window device has been said to derive from Derain.

But this painting seems a little early to be an echo. What Hartley had from Derain — or what Hartley and Derain shared — would be rather a parallelism of development. Jean Cassou might as well have written of Hartley as of Derain that his "career is a series of abrupt turnings." In the search for a language capable of communicating meaning on a public rather than on a private basis, both experimented, as it might seem, endlessly. A Derain touch may be seen, to be sure, in a sort of "scratchboard" technic which occurs in the 1934 *Dogtown* and in the 1936 *Lobster Buoys and Nets*. The often repeated "window" is another matter, revealing a view on life.

Like the pyramid, the window recurs in Hartley's works. It reaches its culmination in *Camden Hills from Baker's Island*, 1938. But even twenty years earlier Hartley was toying with the composition. In 1919 and in 1920 he painted the New Mexican landscape through windows, often with flowering cactus plants on the sill. In the city, he looked through a window to the street, past a rubber plant, to see the faces of two passers-by shadowy through the glass. At Vence he painted still-life compositions set out on a window sill with a distant landscape as background. In 1942 he painted the Smith College *Sea Window, Tinker Mackerel*, with a double and a single perspective, with two-dimensional and three-dimensional space rendering. Till then, for the most part, he had struggled with formal devices and found them incomplete and unsatisfying. He mastered the device when he no longer sought to make form his end rather than his means.

In New Mexico, however, Hartley began his exploration of the new subject matter by working in pastels. Nine of these survive in the Walker Collection, a useful series for studying the creative process in operation. None has been reproduced here because the very fragility of the medium of which Hartley complained prevents it from lending itself to reproduction on equal terms with the heavier tonal weight of oils. The colors are at once brilliant and soft, deep and delicate. The intense, scorching light of the semidesert country and the brilliant, seething colors of the eroded earth moved Hartley to respond in similarly intense, staccato action.

Later, in the south of France, on the Chevreuse, he noted on a sketch in

30

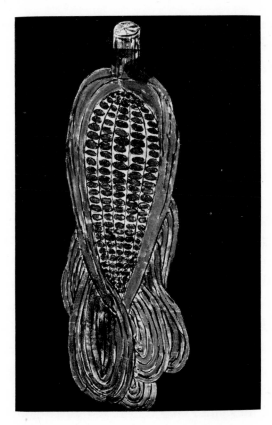

Still Life No. 3. Oil, 14⅛ x 9⅝. 1916.

oils that it has been made in twenty minutes, before the ferocious mos-
quitoes compelled him to leave the scene. In the pastels made near Taos, he
must have worked at great speed, stroking the powdery yet lustrous pig-
ments on the paper before his mood could change. At this point in his development Hartley seems remarkably free from influences. The route between his eye, nature, and what he put down as art is uncomplicated.
Scenes such as *The Little Arroyo, Taos*, 1918, and *Arroyo Hondo, Valdez*,
1918, are recognizable without being representational, as are other of the
New Mexican landscapes recognizable by one who knows the countryside.

Yet by 1920, when he had returned to New York from the Southwest,
after a trip to California and some time spent in Santa Fe, Hartley was once

31

again making use of symbolism, as in *Santos*, a curious fusion of the native Indian folk art objects, *santos bultos*, and the literary manner of his 1913 *One Portrait of One Woman*. The recollection of emotion in tranquility — or in storm and stress — seems always to have affected Hartley in such a manner that his recollections take on a slightly wooden character. At least this is the effect on the author of such a still life as *Floral Life: Debonair*, ingratiating though some aspects of the painting may be.

About this time, either in 1916 or 1917 — and again the data are conflicting — Hartley made the paintings on glass which are the grace notes of his *oeuvre*. It has been suggested that he found a source for these in Bavarian peasant art. However, considering how long the technic was practiced by native folk artists and considering that Hartley has written of his admiration for the American popular art of saloon-window paintings, it seems likely that he was inspired by the American source. Like the "movements" derived from sailboat themes, the paintings on glass are flat in design, and necessarily so, since considerable skill is needed to paint the "top" of the picture first and then to fill in the under-painting from the back.

Apparently with this medium, as with pastel and silver point, Hartley felt that physical difficulties outweighed rewards. By and large he was a painter in oils. His drawings are lively and emphatically sketched in; and his lithographs, probably printed by German craftsmen, are broad and strong. However, except for the 1927 drawings, they lack sensitiveness and flair. Few water colors survive; and pastel, as said before, he gave up because of its fragility. Essentially he favored painting in oils because the medium was one he could control and exploit to the utmost for its material, sensuous qualities of surface and of color.

In this decade Hartley changed his manner of painting not yearly but seasonally. His long habit of painting for a part of the year and then turning to writing for another part of the year had the effect of dividing time into compartments. The considerable amount of travel he was able to afford — in spite of his long-continued financial difficulties — also broke the year up into parts. The result was that his evolution seems at first sight to lack

New Mexico: Landscape. Oil, 18 x 24. 1919.

continuity. He worked, it would appear, by fits and starts, exhausting the interest of a theme or a style, then taking up a new theme or style. At one time he would be preoccupied by grapes, at another by fish; or he would paint thinly with a rapid brush stroke, only to turn back to solid forms.

In general, it is worthwhile to consider the motivation of the "series" in the art of our time. Other painters than Hartley took one theme and worried it to death, so that the idea of theme and variations was not unique with him. The practice smacks not so much of the studio as of the classroom: a set piece is put before the students, and they are instructed to work through all the possible permutations and combinations. With Hartley, as with his contemporary Maurer, the sequence was usually of still lifes — the same vase, compote, or jug appearing with the same mélange of fruits or flowers, but in slightly altered arrangements.

33

562 95

Paysage. Oil, 31¾ x 31¾. 1922.

Before, however, Hartley turned from the still-life compositions of the Southwest to those he painted in Berlin in 1922 and 1923, he sought a catharsis for the trauma of New Mexico. Going back to his beloved Germany on the proceeds of the 1921 auction sale, Hartley painted canvas after canvas of "Recollections of New Mexico." For the most part these large canvases — many of them now taken off their stretchers, rolled up, and put in storage — are painted in a monochromatic palette of gray, relieved with rare touches of green. The forms of nature have been simplified in them, and by a process of emotional montage the remembered shapes of New England have been imposed on the remembered shapes of New Mexico.

Hartley, perhaps more than many, believed that the devils which possess the soul can be exorcised by flight. *Dort, wo du bist nicht, dort ist das Glück* echoes through his letters. Yet in all his journeyings, he found no peace. No place was his place. And each place proved as lonely as the last — An American Place not the least. At the end he found that man's sole strength is in himself. Before he learned this truth, he went many places and saw many places. In memory he saw not the bright and burning fire bush of New Mexico or the brilliant earth hues of arroyo and canyon road but the fore-

34

boding mountain vistas and the stunted tree trunks of a blasted world. Not light but darkness encompassed his vision. Essentially Hartley's heart and eye were centered on nature and his perception of the real world. His recollected world is shadowy and filled with terrors perhaps remembered, perhaps imaginary. Was his reportage of past suffering no more acceptable to him than had been the actuality?

Into his recollections of New Mexico there crept, however, the dream of his 1909 "dark mountain" landscapes and of patriarchal Ryder treading New York's gloomy streets at night. Hartley admired *Wuthering Heights*, he wrote, for its artistry. Yet, consciously or unconsciously, he feared the blighted heath of New Mexico, and to that blighted heath he never returned. How can his mature profound belief that the artist's main source must be found in nature be reconciled with the finical, almost superstitious tone in which he wrote of the suitability or unsuitability of various terrains as subject matter? Again, the variety of his choices of landscape subjects must be considered a reflection of personal associations, whether happy or unhappy, rather than of visual selectivity.

To still life — perhaps as to a finger exercise — he returned again and again. Missing from most of Hartley's still-life paintings is the monumentality of the still lifes of Cézanne, by whom he was early inspired. Hartley's still lifes do, however, have for the most part a suave elegance, a more than competent mastery. He enjoyed painting these arrangements, especially when he might import a touch of nostalgia by including a favorite vase or dish. His domestic treasures were few; his manner of life — moving from one place to another at short intervals — did not encourage him to establish more than a *pied-à-terre*. Yet he cherished some bits of furniture and ceramics, as he wrote a friend. A white compote very like one which the painter Dove gave me years ago appears in the still-life paintings of the years immediately after Hartley's return to Europe. He hoped, he wrote, to have sent to him from Maine a typical "American" rocking chair. Shipping charges proved high, and he was never able to fulfill his dream. But at least he had his dishes, fragments of his native American inheritance.

35

In Germany, in 1923, he turned to the medium of lithography. With the rise of power-press printing and photomechanical methods of reproducing pictorial matter, the handcraft graphic arts had undergone a decline in the United States. Rarely would an artist subject himself to the exemplary disciplines of the metal plate mediums, the woodcut and the wood engraving, and the lithograph. But in the European economy technology came late on the scene, and many skilled handcraftsmen survived. Thus it was not uncommon to find American artists lured by the argument that all the artist needs to do is to draw the composition and let the printer do the rest.

It may be that Hartley drew his stones, "etched" them, and printed them. But this does not seem likely. As late as 1930, he had never packed and crated his paintings, despite his chronic need for funds. So probably he did not choose to undergo the manual labor of the lithographer's craft, but rather made drawings which were transferred to the stone and printed by some small tradesperson. The separation of the design function from the realizing function suggested in such a relation no doubt explains the heavy-handed quality of his lithographs. They are drawn with aesthetic irresponsibility. The lines are heavy and coarse, and conspicuously lacking is the subtle range of tone possible in the lithographic medium when the stone is ground with a fine grain and the artist uses hard lithographic crayons as well as soft. Perhaps Hartley argued that even the least skilled printer cannot lose the outline. Therefore *tant pis*.

Hartley's oils of this period are tentative and groping. Is a composition of three fish on a platter a proposition to be demonstrated like Euclid? How many variations can there be on a theme? Is the search for a style all that concerns the artist? Hartley may, even this early, have felt within himself a turning back to the classical concern of the artist for substance or matter, as well as for style or manner. Yet in the twenties our artists were inextricably implicated in an endeavor to infuse American culture with European aesthetic and intellectual values. In consequence, a man whose bent was toward nature and reality was necessarily pulled in opposite directions. This historical conflict explains the character of Hartley's painting at this

Still Life. Oil, 20 x 24. 1923.

time. His brush stroke has an unsure "feel," as if, after the emphatic sim-
plifications of the New Mexican recollections and of the lithographs of
grapes and other fruits, Hartley could not find which way to turn next. His
working habit was so related to his moods that an inner disaster might keep
him from painting for weeks or months: in 1927 he did not paint at all, he
wrote. After these periods of nonwork, he had to get his hand in again.
In the works of 1922 and 1923 he seems to have sought to reassure himself.
Toward the end of the series he got his material under control, as in the
handsome *Still Life* of 1923 which shows a marked contrast with *Pears in a
White Compote* of the same year. In the latter the emphasis is on a staccato,
febrile surface; in the former, the plastic structures of dish and fruit are
stressed.

On his establishment at Vence in 1924, Hartley returned to what has been called a heavy-handed manner. His early landscapes painted there might be modeled in paint. There is oversimplification of masses, volumes, and planes, not unlike some poster art. This could not have been a question of the locale's natural light, because Hartley wrote of the relatively weak sunlight in the south of France though he also complained of the heat. What artists interested him at the time, I have not yet discovered. Later, of course, he abandoned the hard, chiseled manner of *Landscape, Vence* and turned to Cézanne for inspiration. This happened when he moved to Aix-en-Provence in 1926.

He meant to take up where Cézanne left off, Hartley had announced. But he went back to the Cézannes of the middle 1880s for formal models. He had written that Cézanne lacked a prescribed means and therefore had to invent all things for himself. Hartley was describing his own dilemma and in fact the dilemma of the artist in modern times. There *is* no "prescribed means" for art today; the artist therefore *must* invent his method and his language. The result has been a multiplicity of tongues. The tower of Babel truly symbolizes the communicative confusion of art in a period of multiple patronage. Like many another, Hartley ran from style to style, from manner to manner, seeking to resolve the dilemma, hoping by multiplicity to make himself heard and understood.

This was the impasse of a generation, or perhaps of a century. Previous cultures had commonly accepted symbols and iconographies. Industrial-technological democratic society has not. Concentration on visually perceived external nature thus replaced the content of religious cosmography or of state power. But there was no generally agreed-upon common denominator for the perception of the outer world. There were as many outer worlds as there were pairs of eyes to see. The dwindling of formal, organized patronage threw the artist back on individualism to an increasingly intensified degree. One answer was the retreat from nature and the social world into the personal world, another was solidification and petrifaction of nineteenth-century naturalism into academicism. Between the two, living and creative spirits were almost inevitably forced to choose the former. The interior life became more and more clamorous and insistent, until revolt in the arts reached the pole of abstractionism and nonobjectivity.

Hartley began his career as a pioneer of modern art in America at the beginning of a half-century of change, experiment, and aesthetic controversy. He did not live to see what has been called the academy of the abstract assume a commanding role. If he had, he might have felt that history had passed him by. On the contrary, when abstractionism was still fighting its battle for recognition, in the thirties, Hartley had already turned his back on experimental vanguardism and returned to his first love, nature, by which is meant, of course, a broad view of the visible world, including men and women, other species, the artifacts of man's life on earth, as well as the wonderful procession of the waters upon the earth and the winds and clouds in the sky.

Before he left Vence to invade Cézanne's territory, he had begun to show a freer, fresher eye than had been evident in works like *Landscape, Vence*, 1924/1925. In the valley of the Chevreuse, he painted with a quicker tempo, was less impatient of the subtleties of natural light and form, sought to re-create the "feel" of air and distance. No doubt this change within him turned Hartley to Aix and Cézanne. In the spring of 1927 his friends Charles and Adelaide Kuntz made their way to Aix, only to find that Hartley had preceded them and was established there in a little cottage, called (according to the heading on some of his letters) "Maison Marin — Chateau Noir," which was located on the "Petite Route du Tholonet," post office Aix-en-Provence.

In the new locale, away from the Riviera tourism he deplored, Hartley worked for a new approach. This year he spent drawing, drawing, drawing. Many of these drawings, most of them in silver point, are now in the Hartley estate. In them he took up a problem he had posed himself a score of years earlier in the intertwined birches of the 1908 *Landscape No. 16*. Repeatedly he drew interlocking tree trunks, twisted roots, earth forms of strong geological inspiration. Though he believed that he went beyond Cézanne, it is hard to see that this is true. Rather, from Cézanne he took a method and a way of seeing and put them to use with sympathy and sensitivity.

The year 1928 was broken into early in the spring by a flying trip to the United States, complicated by the difficulties of arranging a common sailing date with friends. At this time Hartley was receiving an income from William C. Bullitt and others; and their contract required clarification. For a few weeks he visited the Bullitts at Conway, Massachusetts, where he painted the rushing mountain brooks of the Berkshires in a spirit reminiscent of his sketches of the French Chevreuse. He also explored Franconia Notch in New Hampshire and visited Gaston and Isabel Lachaise at Georgetown, Maine.

On his return to Europe, late in the summer, he remained in Paris, feeling it would not be worth his while to go to the south of France for a short period. He was, he wrote a friend in the United States, painting sea shells because he needed stable models. He was painting to get his hand and eye back to health, he added. Again in 1935 and 1936 sea subjects served this therapeutic function for Hartley. His subjects for 1928 show considerable variety, as do his styles. As always travel and change of surroundings changed Hartley, at least superficially. Among others, there is a lively series of still lifes of anemones and other garden flowers, of mushrooms, eggplant, endive and garlic, eggs, and the like, which must have been painted in a comparatively brief period of time, for the manner is oddly homogeneous. Later this year he painted Mont-Sainte-Victoire, with a system of broken brush strokes which continued until 1930, as may be seen in *Beaver Lake, Lost River Region.*

In August 1929 Hartley was planning to be back in his native New England by the following spring or summer. History assisted him. The stock market crash of October 29 forcibly repatriated many American intellectuals who had found Europe more congenial than America. Spring found Hartley living in Brooklyn, trying to cure his soul by painting gardenias. He had forgotten the pain of Taos and hoped to be living in the Southwest the following year.

Landscape, Vence.
Oil, 25½ x 31¾. 1924/1925.

Peasants' Paradise.
Oil, 19½ x 24. 1928.

Beaver Lake, Lost River Region. Oil, 35 x 30. 1930.

Meanwhile he found a working place that summer at Franconia, New Hampshire, where he lived exactly as he had lived twenty years before at Center Lovell, Maine. The Franconia region was one from which Hartley reacted with strong emotions, for the known letters of this time reveal lively disgust and ennui.

At the beginning, however, he had written with enthusiasm of the Lost River country; and certainly the example of this series in the Walker Collection, *Beaver Lake,* is a first-rate painting, successfully utilizing the system he had evolved at Aix. Not yet had Hartley returned in spirit to nature as his source: facing nature day and night constantly with no escape was more than he could endure. New England became his Siberia. Not till November 1930 did he manage to return to Brooklyn, where a friend found him so

42

depleted of energy and money that he was unable to get his paintings from the Railway Express Company. A siege of bronchitis followed which laid him up for weeks.

His return to his native land was not attended solely by despair and illness. In March 1931 he was informed that he had been awarded a Guggenheim fellowship. With that curious vanity of his, he wrote he had received "the Guggenheim thing." But he would not, he added, go to the Southwest and Mexico till the end of the year. Rather he would plan a summer of quiet rest and work at Gloucester, where he had always wanted to do a piece of landscape called "Dogtown Common." This theme he managed to paint not only in the summer of 1931, but again in 1934, and once more in 1936. The fantastic shapes of the ancient geological remains of the ice age moraine appealed to his imagination, as did earth forms in New Mexico, Mexico, and the Bavarian Alps.

On the back of *In The Moraine, Dogtown Common, Cape Ann*, 1931, a characteristic example of the series of this year, Hartley has left an inscription which is another clue to his emotional approach to his theme. Partly obliterated and incorrectly quoted and divided into lines, it is from T. S. Eliot's *Ash-Wednesday*, published the year before in London. It reads:

> Teach us to care and not to care
> Teach us to sit still
> Even among these rocks

In his early manhood Hartley had been a devout Episcopalian, as letters to an art-student friend prove. In the last years of his life, he sometimes painted subjects derivative of Christian art. So perhaps it is not strange that he found a "tag" from this American-born exponent of Anglo-Catholicism to use for his painting. Yet if Hartley rejected the obscurantism of Ezra Pound, as some of his correspondence with *Poetry* indicates, one wonders why Eliot's negativistic mysticism was more acceptable. The truth probably is that Hartley himself was torn between contradictory preferences. He wrote once that he liked "aristocrats" and "peasants" but could not stand the middle class. Yet save for his fishermen, his friends were middle-class

43

In the Moraine, Dogtown Common, Cape Ann. Oil, 18 x 24. 1931.

intellectuals, and he apparently found them more understanding of his point of view than either peasants or aristocrats generally would be.

Hartley longed for a bond with humanity, it would seem; yet at the same time, even as Horace did, he hated the vulgar crowd. The evidence for this is that while his letters almost never discuss current political and social issues, he often expressed sentiments which reflect prevailing prejudices against minorities and other oppressed and discriminated-against groups. To a personality so beset with contradictions, the negativism of the Eliot quotation well might be congenial.

Yet as the tragic years of the thirties went by, Hartley underwent a stern education which tempered and chastened his somewhat arrogantly aloof intellectualism. With the majority of American intellectuals who fought a heroic battle to survive in the depression decade, Hartley experienced the

44

reality of having patrons and subsidies wither away. As the years passed, he became not less bitter personally but at least more sensitive to the tragic and heartbreaking depths of life. The three Dogtown series mirror the change. As he grew older and wiser, Hartley felt different meanings emanating from these battered and ruined rock forms.

In 1931 the forms were massive but hard and oversimplified. Indeed the forms of the series of this year are not unrelated to those of the early Vence landscapes, which I have described as cut out of paint. They are literary in quality, or perhaps theatrical, as if confected for stage sets. They show nature not organically but intellectually. By 1934 Hartley's stroke had become more feverish, and the textural use he made of the "scratchboard" technic gave a hurried rhythm to rocks and wind-bent trees. In 1936 he began to brood on the transitory nature of existence.

The Last of the Stone Wall captured his fancy. Man-made form had gone back to earth form. How many stone walls had perished in New England through the slow erosion of time. How many a house in a clearing had yielded to wind and rain. How the years passed over those snow-covered hillsides, inexorable and predatory, letting no human thing survive except at desperate cost. In 1930 Hartley had vowed never to return to New England; in 1931 he began to feel the stir and the pull of his roots. Before he died, those roots would find a new rooting in their native soil.

After Dogtown Hartley went to Mexico in 1932 where he painted, as said before, the volcanic peak of Popocatepetl. The interest of this series is historical and formal rather than expressive. Hartley admired the Mexican art resurgents; and it would seem that in his Mexican period it was Orozco he oversimplified rather than Mexico's sacred mountain. At this time and later, a curious symbolism appears in his painting — of patriarchal figures many times life size, of father and god images, distorted in bulk and character. Was this symbolism a memory of the monumental murals of Orozco, Rivera, and Siqueiros? In Mexico, as at Franconia, Hartley hated the country. But it is obvious that his freely stated revulsion sprang from unfortunate personal experiences rather than from a direct, objective atti-

45

Eight Bells' Folly: Memorial for Hart Crane.
Oil, 31⅝ x 39⅜. 1933.

tude toward the physical fact of the *land* itself. His Popocatepetls, like his early Vence landscapes, are hard and again cut out of paint, flat and clumsy. Yet from them came the synthesis of his Katahdin.

The poet Hart Crane committed suicide during Hartley's stay in Mexico; and as a memorial to his friend, Hartley painted *Eight Bells' Folly*. He had a great fear of death, and in the painting he attempted to resolve his fear, as later he sought to resolve it in *Fishermen's Last Supper*. Hartley, it almost seems, looked after as well as before. He often seemed, as it were, to anticipate himself. Ideas not fully apprehended would swim to the surface of his artistic consciousness and then, perhaps many years later, reveal themselves completed. The shark waits for his victim, the bell buoy tolls farewell, the ghostly schooner sails on frozen waves, while the dark, mourning sky is starred with symbols of mystical signification. This is Hartley's hymn to

46

Garmisch-Partenkirchen. Oil, 29¾ x 22¼. 1933.

death. Later he would sing of death in a music fused with reality, in the paintings of drowned fishermen and dead sea birds.

From Mexico Hartley went to Germany. There he did not hate the land or have to face morbid facts. He had always found life in Germany congenial. The armed fist, the belief that might makes right, that whatever is must be, the overt aspects of junkerism, seem not to have impressed him adversely. Perhaps *Gemütlichkeit* moved him to such an extent that he was unaware of other qualities in German culture. At any rate the oils done in the fall and winter of 1933 and 1934 are among his best. Was the character of life in Bavaria softer and more humane than that of Prussia and Berlin or Königsberg, even though the winter snows lay many feet deep on the Alpine slopes?

At Garmisch-Partenkirchen, he drew and sketched in pastel, planned lithographs of the locale which became the theater of the 1936 Olympic games, and finally painted handsome oils of towering peaks at different times of the fall and winter. These have been called monochromatic; they actually make use of a rich range of color. The 1933 *Garmisch-Partenkirchen* in the Walker Collection shows pines painted in a palette of deep cobalt blues and deep emerald greens mingled with black. The mountains are outlined in ultramarine blue and the sky is painted in ultramarine blue with pinkish-white clouds, while the snow shows gradations of pinkish-gray deepening to strong bluish modeling relieved with areas of Indian red mixed with white. This seems sufficiently colorful. The *Garmisch-Partenkirchen* of 1933/1934 is cooler in palette. The former must have been completed by the middle of October, according to a railway shipping label on the back dated October 18, 1933; the latter probably was painted in the dead of winter, and its color scheme is therefore controlled by the cool but colored whites of snow in sparkling winter light. Brilliant as these are, they seem somewhat detached from the "spine" of Hartley's work. Dazzling spectacles in the pantomime of nature, they stand alone, apart from his main themes. Yet without them, Katahdin could not have been. Was all Hartley's life endeavor but a clearing of the ground for the work of his last years?

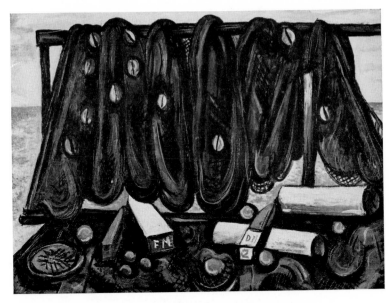

Lobster Buoys and Nets. Oil, 18⅛ x 24. 1936.

Labrador Ducks. Oil, 18 x 24. 1936.

Give Us This Day. Oil, 30 x 40. 1938/1939.

Hartley had ten more years of work ahead of him. He painted in New York and Maine in 1934; and in 1935 he painted in Bermuda and in Nova Scotia, where he began that adventure in spiritual self-rediscovery which culminated magnificently in his last work. Like most artists in the depression years he was in desperate financial straits. His relations with Stieglitz were deteriorating; and the Downtown Gallery had not made many sales for him. If only he could have twenty-five hundred dollars in hand to plan for the next year and a half! In discouragement and frustration he painted many still lifes, fragments of the detritus of existence. Sometimes he managed to break through his anxieties to enjoy the memory of semitropical flora and fauna, of "sky-blue-pink fish." *Dahlias and Crab* and *Squid* show forth all the old Hartley elegance. Going from Bermuda to Nova Scotia in 1935, he found a fisherman's family with whom to live. He paid seven dol-

Fishermen's Last Supper. Oil, 22 x 28. 1938.

Adelard the Drowned, Master
of the *Phantom*. Oil, 28 x 22.
1938/1939.

Marie St. Esprit. Oil,
28 x 22. 1938/1939.

Cleophas, Master of the
Gilda Gray. Oil, 28 x 22.
1938/1939.

lars a week for board and room, with laundry and mending thrown in. The mother was beautiful, and the two giant sons looked like bears but were gentle as lambs. Hartley sketched and drew and comforted his soul in the company of these friendly human beings.

The winter was difficult, he wrote a friend. He asked for employment on the Federal Art Project in New York City and got it. But he hated the paraphernalia of time sheets and time keepers. How long he kept his place on the payroll is uncertain and what happened to the paintings he made for the project is not clear. The rapid liquidation of all the federal temporary "relief" programs at the end of the thirties due to the onset of World War II had as a side-effect not only the dismantling and disbanding of offices and personnel but the hasty disposal of much art work as "government surplus." No doubt important American paintings and sculptures done under these auspices will some day come to light, perhaps in a secondhand dealer's store. It is to be hoped that in such hypothetical circumstances, Hartleys will be found among them.

In spite of economic difficulties, Hartley managed to return to Nova Scotia in 1936. He did not, at that time, make his memorable series of the fisherfolk with whom he lived. His remarkable "archaic" portraits — *Cleophas, Master of the Gilda Gray, Adelard the Drowned, Master of the Phantom, Marie St. Esprit*, and others not in the Walker Collection — were painted from memory in 1938 as Hartley pondered on things past. Instead, in 1936, he painted his third series of Dogtown Common themes, and he began painting marines which show the influence of Ryder, transformed and assimilated. In these works natural forms are not excessively simplified, and they are no longer hard and cut out, nor do they smack of the importation of literary symbols into the painting, as did the 1913 Kandinsky-inspired "movements" and the curious religious symbols of the 1932/1933 Mexican work. Waves, clouds, sky, fishing boats, and rocks on the shore are observed in nature and restated in a personal style.

There seem to be no echoes in this period. Certainly there are none in *Labrador Ducks*, even though Ryder's *Dead Bird* may first have drawn Hartley to the compassionable victims of storm and gale. The fate of the

52

Waterfall, Morse Pond.
Oil, 22 x 28. 1937/1938.

Robin Hood Cove, Georgetown,
Maine. Oil, 22 x 26. 1938/1939.

Camden Hills from Baker's Island, Penobscot Bay. Oil, 28 x 22. 1938.

wild life of the Maine coast was to engross his attention thereafter; and during the last year of his life Hartley felt ever deeper sympathy for the sea birds who could not outwing the tempest. At other times he saw the sunlight of their lives, as in that brilliant painting of mating *Love on the Cliff*, or the inescapable drive of wild creatures to survive, as in *Give Us This Day* "the food by which we may live."

In 1937 Hartley went back to Georgetown, where he had visited the Lachaises almost ten years before and where he had always hoped to return. He was determined, he wrote, to become the first painter of Maine For his exhibition of paintings completed in 1936, held at Stieglitz's An American Place in the spring of 1937, Hartley had written a short essay "On the Subject of Nativeness — a Tribute to Maine." He delivered, in effect, a manifesto with a "Keep Out — Posted" tone, writing: "This quality of nativeness is coloured by heritage, birth, and environment, and it is therefore for this reason that I wish to declare myself the painter from Maine. . . . And so I say to my native continent of Maine, be patient and forgiving, I will soon put my cheek to your cheek, expecting the welcome of the prodigal, and be glad of it, listening all the while to the slow, rich, solemn music of the Androscoggin, as it flows along."

What would be his source now? His letters emphasize his conviction that nature must be the artist's theme. By the fall of 1938 he was able to prove once and for all that his source was nature, including humanity. As he painted his well-loved Nova Scotian family or as he painted Camden Hills from Baker's Island, past became present for Hartley. Now he relied on no outside models for a style, on no fashions in aesthetic theory, not even on his lifelong need to outvie other artists. Now he relied only on the memory of the past and the thought of the future, only on the knowledge of the indestructible virtue of mankind and the eternal persistence of life. The native had come home to himself.

The beauty of Hartley's late work is not alone a sensuous beauty, though truly his color and surface are exquisite in such paintings as *Robin Hood Cove, Camden Hills*, and *Waterfall, Morse Pond*, but a spiritual

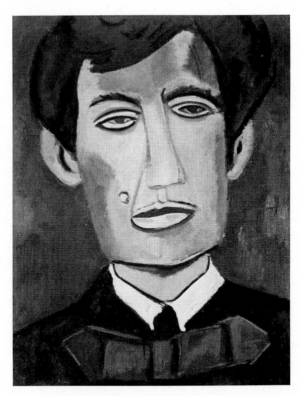

Young Worshipper of the Truth.
Oil, 28 x 22. 1939/1940.

beauty also. The color is glowing and tangible, with dark greens, browns, rusts, posed against the light blues and whites of sky and clouds and against the darker blue of the water. But fundamentally one is not concerned at this point with the painter's materials. It is the ultimate content Hartley has infused into the work which makes a profound aesthetic and emotional impact.

Hartley had at last made his reconcilement with the land of his youth, and perhaps even with his memories of that youth. His native continent had claimed him, and he had claimed his native continent. The Androscoggin flowed slowly, richly, solemnly, for him now. No longer a prodigal or an outcast, Hartley was free from the tyranny of incessantly changing styles by which he had sought to find his place in the world. At his command he had

Mt. Katahdin.
Oil, 30 x 40. 1942.

that variety of manners with which he had, as it were, played during the long, slow, painful years of his coming of age, of his coming home. Dignity and power could replace elegance because Hartley no longer feared to be himself. The material success he had late in life aided his emotional emancipation. Fear no longer rode him. He had money in the bank. He had recognition. He had friends. He had a spiritual home. The creative effects are clear in his last paintings.

Ryder was no longer his master, but his equal, Hartley's memory portrait says. He could find inspiration in the American past to salute that great good man, Lincoln, or to imagine him as the beardless *Young Worshipper of the Truth*. Finally the triangle ceased to be a mechanically oversimplified compositional device and became reality. In the poverty-stricken days of the 1900s when he was lucky to have four dollars a week to live on, Hartley had managed to buy Japanese prints. Freed from compulsive rivalry and jealousy, Hartley could draw and paint Katahdin a thousand times and feel no sense of competition with Hiroshige. The paintings therefore are free.

Finally he painted roses for sea gulls that lost their way at sea, but he painted roses for joy also, as in *Flowers from Lachaise's Garden*. Even if

57

Dead Plover. Oil, 16 x 20. 1942/1943.

he was ill or ailing that last winter of 1942/1943, when he painted dead sea birds again and again, his pity was for them, not for himself. And if he thought of death as it might concern him, yet he surely did not paint his last canvas, *Roses*, in a mood of self-pity. Life must end, but in a splendid efflorescence of glory.

III

Hartley's flowering was late but rich. It would have been richer and ever more intense if death had not come prematurely. Yet though brief its time was and necessarily restricted its extent, the flowering was brilliant. Hartley's late blooming justified all the trial and error that had gone before. For what he said at last became a tremendous paean to the human hunger to be creative, no matter how forbidding the circumstances of existence may be. The hostilities, antagonisms, jealousies, rivalries, emotions of insecurity and persecution which harried Hartley all his life, were resolved in a final, utter capacity to be the observer, but to be also, and especially, the poet in words and visual images of human thought and feeling, of suffering and pain and death, but of triumph also.

To attain the goal he had been searching for all his life, Hartley broke the mirror of style. He ceased to be imitator, emulator, experimenter. He became spokesman, expresser of experience. He spoke of the tragedy of life, but with the nobility of catharsis. His theme was often the tears of things, but the tears were true, whether for drowned fishermen or dead plover. He had learned that art is not a game or a window display, not an exhibition or a circus, but man's way of proving that life is purposive, that the eternal Nay cannot forever defeat the eternal Yea. By his *Stirb und Werde* Hartley became, not a dismal guest on a gloomy earth, but a native of the world he looked upon and found lovely and good.

Thus Hartley joined himself not alone to the company of the dead but to the company of the living, not alone to drowned fishermen and dead sea birds but to those who have spoken most deeply and meaningfully of the relation between man and the physical universe in which he moves and has his being. Ryder, Hartley had acknowledged first as master, then as peer. Homer became his fellow, too, by Hartley's act if not by his confession. Perhaps more than the painters of any other time and place — except the Renaissance when space liberated the mind and maps became high art — have American artists been inspired by the excitement and allure of limitless land and limitless horizons. Within the narrow world of his opportunity, as he felt it to be, Hartley sought an expanding land, an expanding frontier, even as we today dream of an expanding galactic universe. Uniting himself with his native continent, Hartley united himself with the American past which dreamed of free land, free space, uncorrupted nature. Enriching American naturalism with his fresh view of the world, Hartley became in his turn master, peer, and fellow of American artists yet to come. The circle was complete.

Roses. Oil, 40 x 30. 1943.

CHECK LIST, CHRONOLOGY, AND BIBLIOGRAPHY

CHECK LIST

DATING Hartley's work is complicated by the fact that the artist seldom signed and dated his paintings on their faces. Notations on the back of some of them may, or may not, have been made contemporaneously with the work. In his later years Hartley worked at times on pictures from the summer or fall of one year to the early spring of the next, when he would exhibit them with a split date. The question is further complicated because Hartley as a man of his time — a time fragmented by aesthetic variety — passed through many styles in a short period. Similarity of subject matter is also deceiving because the superficial identity of objects such as flowers, fruits, fish, shells, and vases may mask vital differences of style. The system here is provisional and subject to revision after extended study of the Hartley letters and papers, as well as of the works themselves.

The basic test of internal evidence has been substantiated by external documentation. However, if paintings have been signed and/or dated on the back, in Hartley's hand, these dates have been accepted for the time being, with the reservation that an artist may err in matters of fact like dates unless he signs and dates the work at the time it is completed. Lacking a statement from the artist, either on the front or on the back of the picture, the author has used exhibition and auction sale catalogues for corroboration of stylistic criteria. Since 1944, when the Museum of Modern Art held its Feininger-Hartley exhibition, the American Art Research Council has made a record of almost a thousand Hartleys, which was generously made available for this study. These data have made necessary changes in some of the dates given in that exhibition's catalogue, as has study of contemporary press accounts and of Hartley letters kindly made accessible by old friends of the artist. Further study must be made, however, before a definitive system of dating can be hoped for.

To differentiate, dates derived from the artist's signature on the face of the work are given in the righthand column without any distinguishing mark, as for example "1923"; dates derived from signatures on the back are enclosed in parentheses, as "(1916)"; and attributed dates are enclosed in brackets, as "[1908]." The dates in the lefthand margin are for the reader's convenience in studying the development of Hartley's styles by years. Sizes are given in inches, height first. For drawings, prints, pastels, and water colors, the size is the full paper size, except for framed works, for which the dimensions are those of the frame's opening, a fact indicated by "(sight)." Split dates are denoted by the use of the oblique stroke, as "1923/1924."

ante 1909   FRAGMENT OF A NUDE   [*ca.* 1900]
Oil on cardboard, 13¼ x 16¼, unsigned

LANDSCAPE NO. 29   (1907?)
Oil on wood, 9⅝ x 5¼, unsigned

AUTUMN   [1908]
Oil on canvas, 30 x 30, unsigned

AUTUMN   [1908]
Oil on academy board, 12 x 14, unsigned

BRANCH OF BIRCH   ⌊1908]
Water color and pencil on paper, 12 x 9, signed lower left, *Marsden Hartley*; also *branch of birch* (erased); lower right, *M H* (in monogram)

CARNIVAL OF AUTUMN   [1908]
Oil on canvas, 30¼ x 30⅛, unsigned

HILLS   [1908]
Oil on academy board, 12 x 12, unsigned

LANDSCAPE   [1908]
Oil on academy board, 12 x 12, unsigned

LANDSCAPE NO. 16   [1908]
Oil on academy board, 11⅞ x 8⅞, unsigned

LANDSCAPE NO. 18   [1908]
Oil on academy board, 12 x 12, unsigned

LATE AUTUMN   [1908]
Oil on academy board, 12 x 14, unsigned

LATE AUTUMN   [1908]
Oil on academy board, 12 x 14, signed lower left, toward center, *MARSDEN HARTLEY*

MAINE SNOWSTORM   [1908]
Oil on canvas, 30 x 30, unsigned

OLD MAID KNITTING   [1908]
Pencil on paper, 12 x 9, signed lower left, *Marsden Hartley*; lower right, *Old Maid / Knitting*

OLD MAN IN A ROCKING CHAIR   1908
Pencil on paper, 12 x 9, signed lower left, *Marsden Hartley / 1908*

SELF-PORTRAIT   [1908]
Pencil on paper, 12 x 9, signed lower left, *Marsden Hartley*

SONGS OF WINTER   [1908]
Oil on academy board, 9 x 12, signed lower right, *MARSDEN HART-LEY* (in black paint)

STORM CLOUDS, MAINE   [1908]
Oil on canvas, 30½ x 25½, signed lower right, *Edmund Marsden Hartley* ("Edmund" and "Marsden" are in capital and small capitals, "Hartley" in upper and lower case)

SUMMER   [1908]
Oil on academy board, 9 x 12, signed lower left, *MARSDEN HARTLEY*

ante 1909	TREE	[1908]

Water color and pencil on paper, 12 x 9, signed lower left, *M H* (in monogram); lower right, *Marsden Hartley*

TREES IN AUTUMN [1908]
Oil on academy board, 12 x 14, unsigned

1909   BATHERS (1909)
Oil on academy board, 9 x 9, unsigned

DESERTED FARM [1909]
Oil on composition board, 24 x 20, signed lower left, *MARSDEN HART-LEY* (in black paint)

LANDSCAPE NO. 10 [1909]
Oil on wood, 9⅜ x 5¼, unsigned

LANDSCAPE NO. 14 (1909)
Oil on academy board, 12 x 14, unsigned

LANDSCAPE NO. 28 (1909)
Oil on academy board, 14 x 12, unsigned

LANDSCAPE NO. 36 [1909]
Oil on canvas, 30⅛ x 34, unsigned

MOUNTAINSIDE [1909]
Oil on academy board, 12 x 14, unsigned

WATERFALL [1909]
Oil on academy board, 12 x 12, unsigned

WOODS [1909]
Oil on academy board, 12 x 14, unsigned

1910   STILL LIFE NO. 12 [1910]
Oil on canvas, 20 x 16, unsigned

1911   ABSTRACTION [1911]
Oil on cardboard, 16¼ x 13¼, unsigned

LANDSCAPE NO. 32 (1911)
Water color on paper, 14⅛ x 10, unsigned

PEARS [1911]
Oil on wood, 16 x 12¼, signed lower right, *MARSDEN HARTLEY* (in black paint)

STILL LIFE: FRUIT [1911]
Oil on canvas, 20 x 20¼, signed lower right, *M. H.* (in black paint)

STILL LIFE NO. 11 [1911]
Oil on canvas, 9½ x 7½, unsigned

1912   STILL LIFE (1912)
Oil on composition board, 32⅛ x 25⅝, unsigned

1913   FORMS ABSTRACTED (1913)
Oil on canvas, 39 x 31¼, unsigned

MILITARY [1913]
Oil on canvas, 39¼ x 39¼, unsigned

| 1913 | ABSTRACTION WITH FLOWERS | [1913] |

Oil on canvas, 39½ x 31½, unsigned

MOVEMENTS [1913]

Oil on canvas, 39½ x 31½, unsigned

ONE PORTRAIT OF ONE WOMAN [1913]

Oil on compo-board, 30 x 25¼, unsigned

PAINTING NO. 1 (1913)

Oil on canvas, 39⅜ x 31⅞, unsigned

PAINTING NO. 2 (1913)

Oil on canvas, 39¼ x 31¾, unsigned

STILL LIFE WITH FLOWERS (1913)

Oil on wood, 16 x 11¾, unsigned

1914/1915 BERLIN ABSTRACTION [1914/1915]

Oil on canvas, 32 x 26, unsigned

PORTRAIT [1914/1915]

Oil on canvas, 31¾ x 21⅛, unsigned

1916 A BERMUDA WINDOW IN A SEMITROPIC CHARACTER [1916]

Oil on composition board, 31¾ x 26, unsigned

MOVEMENT NO. 3, PROVINCETOWN (1916)

Oil on beaver board, 19⅞ x 15⅞, unsigned

MOVEMENT NO. 9 [1916]

Oil on composition board, 24⅛ x 20⅛, unsigned

STILL LIFE NO. 3 (1916)

Oil on glass, 14⅛ x 9⅜ (sight), unsigned

1917 ELSA (1917)

Oil on composition board, 20⅛ x 16, unsigned

ELSA KOBENHAVN [1917]

Oil on composition board, 24 x 20, unsigned

MOVEMENT NO. 11 [1917]

Oil on composition board, 19½ x 15½, unsigned

1918 ARROYO HONDO, VALDEZ 1918

Pastel on cardboard, 17¼ x 27⅝, signed lower right, *Marsden Hartley / Arroyo Hondo / Valdez / 1918.* (in ink)

LANDSCAPE, NEW MEXICO [1918]

Pastel on paper, 22⅛ x 16⅝, unsigned

LANDSCAPE NO. 12 1918

Pastel on cardboard, 17½ x 27⅞, signed lower left, *Marsden Hartley / 1918.* (in ink)

THE LITTLE ARROYO, TAOS 1918

Pastel on paper, 16½ x 27 (sight), signed lower left, *The little Arroyo — Taos. / Marsden Hartley / 1918.* (in ink)

NEW MEXICO 1918

Pastel on cardboard, 17⅝ x 28¼, signed lower left, *Marsden Hartley / 1918.* (in ink)

1918 NEW MEXICO [1918]
Pastel on paper, 17 x 27½ (sight), unsigned

NEW MEXICO: LANDSCAPE [1918]
Pastel on paper, about 12 x 18 (irregular in shape), signed lower center, *Marsden Hartley*

STILL LIFE NO. 5 1918
Pastel on cardboard, 27⅞ x 17½, signed lower right, *Marsden Hartley / 1918.* (in ink)

1919 LANDSCAPE NO. 8 1919
Pastel on cardboard, 17⅜ x 28, signed lower right, *Marsden Hartley / 1919.* (in ink)

NEW MEXICO: LANDSCAPE [1919]
Oil on canvas, 18 x 24, unsigned

1920 FLORAL LIFE: DEBONAIR 1920
Oil on canvas, 22 x 16, signed lower right, *MARSDEN HARTLEY / 1920* (in pink paint)

LANDSCAPE: NEW MEXICO [1920]
Oil on composition board, 25½ x 29¾, unsigned

SANTOS: NEW MEXICO [1920]
Oil on composition board, 31⅝ x 23⅝, unsigned

STILL LIFE NO. 7 [1920]
Oil on canvas board, 16 x 12, unsigned

STILL LIFE NO. 9 [1920]
Oil on beaver board, 24 x 20, unsigned

STILL LIFE, NO. ——— [illegible on the back] [1920]
Oil on canvas, 32 x 24, unsigned

WESTERN FLAME 1920
Oil on canvas, 22 x 31¾, signed lower right, *MARSDEN HARTLEY / 1920* (in blue paint)

1922 PAYSAGE [1922]
Oil on canvas, 31¾ x 31¾, signed lower center, *M. H.* (in black paint, in a circle)

RUBBER PLANT [1922]
Oil on canvas, 28 x 25, unsigned

1923 APPLES AND PEARS 1923
Lithograph on paper 15½ x 20½, signed lower right, *Marsden Hartley 1923* (in pencil)

BASKET AND NAPKIN (1923)
Oil on canvas, 13⅝ x 25½, unsigned

BOWL OF FRUIT 1923
Lithograph on paper, 17½ x 15, signed lower right, *Marsden Hartley / 1923* (in pencil)

GRAPES 1923
Lithograph on paper, 13½ x 15½, signed lower right, *Marsden Hartley 1923*

1923 GRAPES ON PLATTER 1923
Lithograph on paper, 15½ x 20, signed lower right, *Marsden Hartley / 1923*

PEARS IN A WHITE COMPOTE [1923]
Oil on canvas, 21¼ x 25½, unsigned

PEARS, NO. 3 [1923]
Lithograph on paper, 12½ x 18½, signed lower right, *Marsden Hartley*

POMEGRANATE, PEAR, AND APPLE 1923
Lithograph on paper, 15½ x 17⅝, signed lower right, *Marsden Hartley 1923*

STILL LIFE (1923)
Oil on canvas, 20 x 24 (sight), unsigned

THREE BLUE FISH WITH LEMONS AND LIMES [1922/1923]
Oil on canvas, 10⅝ x 18½, unsigned

THREE RED FISH [1923]
Oil on canvas, 10½ x 18 (sight), unsigned

THREE RED FISH WITH LEMONS [1923]
Oil on canvas, 13½ x 25½ (sight), unsigned

1924 STILL LIFE NO. 14 [1924]
Oil on canvas, 22 x 28, unsigned

1925 LANDSCAPE, VENCE [1924/1925]
Oil on canvas, 25½ x 31¾, unsigned

1926 STILL LIFE WITH ARTICHOKE [1925/1926]
Oil on canvas, 13¾ x 25¾, unsigned

1927 STILL LIFE 1927
Pencil on paper, 18⅛ x 23⅞ (sight), signed lower right, *Marsden Hartley / 27* (written with the crossed French figure)

1928 PEASANTS' PARADISE [1928]
Oil on canvas, 19½ x 24, signed lower right, *MARSDEN HARTLEY* (in brown paint)

STILL LIFE NO. 17 [1928]
Oil on wood, 11⅝ x 11⅜, unsigned

1930 BEAVER LAKE, LOST RIVER REGION (1930)
Oil on canvas, 35 x 30, unsigned

1931 IN THE MORAINE, DOGTOWN COMMON, CAPE ANN (1931)
Oil on academy board, 18 x 24, unsigned

WHALE'S JAW, DOGTOWN [1931]
Charcoal on paper, 13 x 16, unsigned

WHALE'S JAW, DOGTOWN, 2 [1931]
Charcoal on paper, 13 x 16, unsigned

1933 ALPINE MOTIVE 1933
Sepia ink on paper, 7⅛ x 10⅛, signed lower left, *Marsden Hartley / Oct 27–33.*

| 1933 | ALPINE MOTIVE V | 1933 |

Sepia ink on paper, 7⅛ x 5¼, signed lower left, *Marsden Hartley / Oct 27–33.*

ALPINE MOTIVE VI [1933]

Sepia ink on paper, 5¼ x 7⅞, unsigned

ALPSPITZE, GARMISCH-PARTENKIRCHEN [1933]

Pastel on gray paper, 15½ x 18¼, unsigned

ALPSPITZE, GARMISCH-PARTENKIRCHEN [1933]

Pastel on rose paper, 8¾ x 11⅞, unsigned

EIGHT BELLS' FOLLY: MEMORIAL FOR HART CRANE (1933)

Oil on canvas, 31⅝ x 39⅝, unsigned

GARMISCH-PARTENKIRCHEN [1933]

Charcoal on paper, 13¼ x 10, unsigned

GARMISCH-PARTENKIRCHEN [1933]

Oil on composition board, 29¾ x 22¼, unsigned

STUDY FOR GARMISCH-PARTENKIRCHEN SERIES [1933]

Crayon, 13¼ x 10, unsigned

WAXENSTEIN 1933

Lithograph on paper, 16 x 11, signed lower left, *Waxenstein / 50*; lower right, *Marsden Hartley / 1923*

THE WAXENSTEIN, GARMISCH-PARTENKIRCHEN [1933]

Pastel on gray paper, 20 x 15¼, unsigned

1934 ALPSPITZE 1934

Lithograph on paper, 15⅞ x 23⅜, signed lower left, *# 5 Alpspitz* (an error on the artist's part); lower right, *Marsden Hartley / 1934* (in one line) (both in pencil)

DREITORSPITZE [1934]

Lithograph on paper, 16 x 23¾, signed lower left, *Dreitorspitz* (an error on the artist's part); lower right, *Marsden Hartley* (both in pencil)

GARMISCH-PARTENKIRCHEN [1933/1934]

Oil on composition board, 19⅞ x 29⅝ (sight), unsigned

KOPELBERG, OBERAMMERGAU 1934

Lithograph on paper, 19⅝ x 15⅝, signed lower left, *# 10 Kopelberg, Oberammergau*; lower right, *Marsden Hartley / 1934* (in one line) (both in pencil)

DOGTOWN [1934]

Oil on masonite, 15⅞ x 28¾, unsigned

1936 DAHLIAS AND CRAB [1936]

Oil on canvas board, 18 x 14, unsigned

DOGTOWN [1936]

Charcoal on paper, 12¾ x 16, unsigned

DOGTOWN COMMON [1936]

Oil on academy board, 9¼ x 13, unsigned

1936   DOGTOWN COMMON   [1936]
       Oil on academy board, 8 x 10, unsigned

       DOGTOWN, THE LAST OF THE STONE WALL   [1936]
       Oil on academy board, 18 x 24, signed lower right, *M. H*

       FISHING BOAT IN A STORM   [1936]
       Oil on canvas board, 14 x 18, unsigned

       GLOUCESTER SHORE   [1936]
       Pencil on paper, 5¼ x 8¼, unsigned

       LABRADOR DUCKS   [1936]
       Oil on academy board, 18 x 24, unsigned

       LOBSTER BUOYS AND NETS   [1936]
       Oil on academy board, 18⅛ x 24, unsigned

       THE OLD BARS, DOGTOWN   [1936]
       Ink on paper, 10⅛ x 13⅛, unsigned

       ROPE AND SHELLS   [1936]
       Oil on academy board, 16 x 12, unsigned

       SHELLS   [1936]
       Ink on paper, 14½ x 11⅜, unsigned

       SHELLS AND WISHBONES   [1936]
       Ink and gouache on gray cardboard, 15 x 10, unsigned

       SQUID   [1936]
       Oil on academy board, 12 x 16, unsigned

       WHALE'S JAW   [1936]
       Crayon on paper, 12¾ x 16, unsigned

       WILD SEA ROSE   [1936]
       Water color and gouache on pink paper, 8¼ x 13 (sight), signed lower
       right, *Marsden Hartley / For Ione Walker* (apparently added later)

1937   BY THE SEA   [1937]
       Lithographic crayon and white chalk on gray cardboard, 18¾ x 25⅞,
       unsigned

       FISHING SHACK AND LOBSTER POTS   [1937]
       Lithographic crayon and white chalk on gray cardboard, 18¾ x 25⅞,
       unsigned

       FISHING VILLAGE   [1937]
       Lithographic crayon and white chalk on gray cardboard, 10¼ x 26,
       unsigned

       LIGHTHOUSE   [1937]
       Lithographic crayon on paper, 12 x 14, unsigned

       NEW ENGLAND FISHERMAN   [1937]
       Lithographic crayon on gray cardboard, 26 x 10⅛, unsigned

       PENOBSCOT(?)   [1937]
       Lithographic crayon on paper, 12 x 14, unsigned

1937	SWIMMING CHAMP	[1937]

1937   SWIMMING CHAMP   [1937]
Lithographic crayon and white chalk on gray cardboard, 10⅛ x 26, unsigned

WATERFALL, MORSE POND   [1937]
Lithographic crayon on paper, 12 x 14, unsigned

1938   CAMDEN HILLS FROM BAKER'S ISLAND,
PENOBSCOT BAY   [1938]
Oil on academy board, 28 x 22, unsigned

FISHERMEN'S LAST SUPPER (first version)   (1938)
Oil on academy board, 22 x 28, unsigned

FLOWERS FROM LACHAISE'S GARDEN   [1937/1938]
Oil on academy board, 24 x 18, unsigned

ISLAND IN PENOBSCOT BAY   [1938]
Oil on academy board, 22 x 28, signed lower left, *M. H.*

WATERFALL, MORSE POND   [1937/1938]
Oil on academy board, 22 x 28, unsigned

1939   ADELARD THE DROWNED, MASTER OF THE *PHANTOM*
     (1938/1939)
Oil on academy board, 28 x 22, unsigned

CHINESE SEA HORSE   [1938/1939]
Oil on academy board, 24 x 18, unsigned

CLEOPHAS, MASTER OF THE *GILDA GRAY*   [1938/1939]
Oil on academy board, 28 x 22, unsigned

FINNISH-YANKEE SAUNA   [1938/1939]
Oil on academy board, 24 x 18, unsigned

FINNISH-YANKEE WRESTLER   [1938/1939]
Oil on academy board, 24 x 18, unsigned

GIVE US THIS DAY   [1938/1939]
Oil on canvas, 30 x 40, unsigned

MARIE ST. ESPRIT   (1938/1939)
Oil on academy board, 28 x 22, unsigned

NORTH ATLANTIC HARVEST   [1938/1939]
Oil on academy board, 18 x 24, signed lower left, *M. H.*

ROBIN HOOD COVE, GEORGETOWN, MAINE   (1938/1939)
Oil on academy board, 22 x 26, signed lower left, *M H.*

1940   DEAD PLOVER   1940
Lithographic crayon and brown crayon and chalk on gray paper, 17¾ x 11¾, signed lower right, *M H / 40.*

DEAD PLOVER   1940
Pastel on gray cardboard, 10⅛ x 26, signed lower right, *M. H. / 40.*

YOUNG WORSHIPPER OF THE TRUTH   [1939/1940]
Oil on academy board, 28 x 22

1941	COBB'S CAMP, LAKE KATAHDIN	[1940/1941]
	Lithographic crayon on paper, 14 x 12, unsigned	
	MT. KATAHDIN	[1940/1941]
	Lithographic crayon on paper, 12 x 14, unsigned	
1942	ACROSS CENTRAL PARK, NEW YORK	[1942]
	Lithographic crayon on paper, 14 x 17, unsigned	
	ACROSS CENTRAL PARK, NEW YORK	[1942]
	Lithographic crayon on paper, 17 x 13¾, unsigned	
	THE CLOISTERS, NEW YORK	[1942]
	Lithographic crayon on paper, 17 x 13¾, unsigned	
	MT. KATAHDIN	1942
	Oil on masonite, 30 x 40, signed lower right, *M.H. / 42.*	
1943	DEAD PLOVER	(1942/1943)
	Oil on masonite, 16 x 20, unsigned	
	ROSES	[1943]
	Oil on canvas, 40 x 30, unsigned	

CHRONOLOGY

1877	January 4: Born at Lewiston, Maine
1892	Cleveland. Studied art with John Semon, Cullen Yates, Nina Waldeck, and Caroline Sowers
1894?	Visited George Inness (in New York?)
1898/1899	New York. Studied at Chase school with William Merritt Chase, Frank Vincent Du Mond, and F. Luis Mora
1900	Late spring and summer: Lewiston Fall and winter: New York. Studied at National Academy of Design with Frances C. Jones, Edgar M. Ward, George Maynard, Edwin H. Blashfield, F. J Dillman, and Inness' son-in-law, F. Scott Hartley
1901	Summer: North Bridgton, Maine. Thereafter spent summers near Center Lovell, Maine, and winters in New York
1908	About this time began painting impressionist landscapes
1909	May 8–18: First one-man exhibition, Photo-Secession Gallery, 291 Fifth Avenue, New York. The Segantini "stitch"
1910	March: In group of younger American painters, at 291, including Dove, Maurer, Carles, Marin, Steichen, and Weber. The Ryder influence
1911	March and April: Cézanne and Picasso, at 291. A new influence for Hartley
1912	February 7–26: Second one-man show at 291. Still lifes in cubist and fauve manners of blue jugs, cucumbers, bananas, and pears Late spring: To Paris. The impact of "modern art"
1913	February 15–March 15: The Armory Show Late fall: Made visit to the United States
1914	January 12–February 14: Third one-man show at 291, comprising "the work done, during the past two years . . . in Paris and Berlin" July 4: In Berlin, painting "prewar pageants"
1915	February: Exhibited at Daniel Gallery October: Work shown at house of Max Liebermann, Berlin December: Returned to the United States
1916	March: Represented in Forum Exhibition by Kandinsky-esque paintings of 1912/1913 April: Exhibited at 291 Visited Provincetown and Bermuda
1916/1917	Began paintings on glass, inspired by American folk-art saloon-window paintings

73

1917	January: Exhibited at 291
	At work in Ogunquit, Maine
1918	June: Left New York for New Mexico. Worked in Taos till mid-November, then to Santa Fe. Art work confined to pastels and drawings
1919	Spring: California, then returned to Santa Fe
	Late fall: To the East. Began oils of New Mexican landscape
1920	Spring: New York
	April: Exhibited at Montross Gallery
	Summer: Gloucester
	Included in Société Anonyme's fifth exhibition
1921	May 21: Auction of Hartley paintings at Anderson Galleries, New York
	Returned to Europe on proceeds of sale
1922/1923	In Berlin, painting recollections of New Mexican landscape, with echoes of 1909 Ryder manner; also, still-life subjects
	Visited Vienna, Florence, Arezzo, Rome
1923	First book of poetry published: *Twenty-Five Poems*, Paris
1924	To Vence
1925	Before September 25: Was established at "Petite Maison" le Paradon, Chemin des Meilliéres, Vence
	Continued painting still life and landscape
1926	March: Exhibited at the Intimate Gallery, New York
	Later removed to Aix-en-Provence from Vence; began painting Mont-Sainte-Victoire, thinking to take up where Cézanne left off
1927	Spring: Found established at Maison Marin, Chateau Noir, Aix
	Fall: In Paris
1928	March: Exhibited at the Arts Club, Chicago
	Spring: To the United States for a business trip
	Early summer: Visited the William C. Bullitts at Conway, Massachusetts, and the Gaston Lachaises at Georgetown, Maine
	Fall: Back to Paris, painting sea shells
1929	January: Exhibited at the Intimate Gallery
	Spring through fall: At Aix again, painting only still lifes
	Flying trip to London for Christmas
1930	Returned to the United States in the early spring and lived at 42 Livingston Street, Brooklyn
	Early summer to mid-November: Franconia, New Hampshire, painting mountain subjects
	December: Exhibited at An American Place, New York
1931	Winter and spring: Lived at 639 East 12th Street, New York, where he wrote sketches of life in Tompkins Square
	Summer and fall: Gloucester, and the first Dogtown Common series
1932	Winter and spring: New York
	April 26–May 15: Exhibited at the Downtown Gallery, New York
	August 24: Left for Mexico on the Guggenheim fellowship awarded in 1931
	Fall: In Cuernavaca and Mexico, D.F., painting Popocatepetl series and symbolic canvases
1933	February: Exhibited at Galeria de la Escuela Central de Artes Plasticas, Mexico, D.F.

1933	To Germany, where he went to Bavaria and painted the Garmisch-Partenkirchen series
1934	Returned to the United States; worked in New York and Maine, notably the second (or "red") Dogtown series
1935	Spring: New York
	Summer: Bermuda
	Fall: Nova Scotia
1936	Winter: New York, where he found employment briefly on the Works Progress Administration Federal Art Project
	March 22–April 14: Exhibited at An American Place
	Summer: Returned to Nova Scotia, painting third Dogtown series
1937	Winter: New York
	April 20–May 17: Exhibited at An American Place, with a regionalist manifesto called "On The Subject of Nativeness — a Tribute to Maine"
	Summer and fall: Georgetown, Maine, painting landscape, notably waterfalls
1938	Winter: New York
	February 28–April 2: First exhibition at Hudson D. Walker Gallery, New York
	Summer and fall: Maine, where he began the Vinalhaven series and the "archaic portraits" of Nova Scotian fisherfolk
	September: Exhibited at Carlin Gallery, Philadelphia
1939	Winter: New York
	March 6–April 8: Exhibited at Hudson D. Walker Gallery
	Summer and fall: Spent in Bangor, Portland, West Brooksville, Maine, including Bagaduce Farm, continuing his program to be the first painter of Maine
	December to January 1940: Exhibited at Symphony Hall, Boston
1940	Late winter: New York
	January 28–February 10: Louisiana State College, Baton Rouge
	March 11–30: Exhibited at Hudson D. Walker Gallery
	March–April: Exhibited at Witte Memorial Museum, San Antonio, Texas
	May 1–19: Exhibited at Portland (Oregon) Art Museum
	July 5–August 6: Exhibited at California Palace of the Legion of Honor, San Francisco
	September 15–October 15: Exhibited at University of Nebraska, Lincoln
	November: Exhibited at Walker Art Center, Minneapolis
	Summer and fall: Corea, Maine
1941	Remained in Maine at least as late as February 15
	In Maine again in the summer and fall
	October 24–November 24: Exhibited (with Stuart Davis) at the Cincinnati Modern Art Society, Cincinnati, in his first retrospective since the 1921 sale
1942	Winter and spring: New York
	February 2–27: First exhibition at Paul Rosenberg & Co., New York
	March 9–28: Exhibited at Macbeth Gallery, New York
	Summer and fall: Corea
	October 12–31: Early drawings shown at Knoedler Galleries, New York
1943	Winter and spring: New York
	September 2: Died at Ellsworth, Maine

BIBLIOGRAPHY

1909   "Paintings by Marsden Hartley." *Camera Work*, July, p. 51.
        CAFFIN, CHARLES H. "Unphotographic Paint: – The Texture of Impression-
        ism." *Camera Work*, October, pp. 20–23.
1910   "Younger American Painters." *Camera Work*, July, pp. 43–49.
1912   "Exhibition of Paintings by Marsden Hartley." *Camera Work*, April, pp. 36–46.
        KANDINSKY, WASSILY. "Excerpts from *The Spiritual in Art.*" *Camera Work*,
        July, pp. 34ff.
        KANDINSKY, WASSILY. *Über das Geistige in der Kunst.* Munich.
1913   ADAMS, ADELINE. "The Secret of Life." *Art and Progress*, April, pp. 925–32.
        ASSOCIATION OF AMERICAN PAINTERS AND SCULPTORS. *International Exhibition
        of Modern Art.* New York. (Catalogue of the so-called Armory Show, held in
        New York, February 15 to March 15.)
        BRINTON, CHRISTIAN. "Evolution Not Revolution." *International Studio*, April,
        pp. xxvii–xxxv.
        CAFFIN, CHARLES H. "As Hartley Sees and Feels It." *New York American*,
        December 22.
        "Lawless Art." *Art and Progress*, April, pp. 940–41.
        "Modern Painting." *International Studio*, March, pp. ix–x.
1914   "Exhibitions at '291.' Exhibition of Recent Paintings by Marsden Hartley."
        Camera Work, January, pp. 16–23.
        HARTLEY, MARSDEN. "What Is 291?" *Camera Work*, July, pp. 35–36.
        KANDINSKY, WASSILY. *The Art of Spiritual Harmony.* London.
1915   DANIEL GALLERY, New York. *Paintings by Marsden Hartley. "The Mountain
        Series."*
1916   *Forum Exhibition of Modern American Painters.* New York. (Catalogue of the
        Forum Exhibition, March 13–25.)
        "Hartley Exhibition." *Camera Work*, October, p. 12.
        Excerpts from the New York art press. *Ibid.*, pp. 58–60.
1918   HARTLEY, MARSDEN. "After Battle." *Poetry*, January, p. 4.
        HARTLEY, MARSDEN. "Kaleidoscope." *Poetry*, July, pp. 195–201.
        HARTLEY, MARSDEN. "Tribal Esthetics." *Dial*, November 16, pp. 399–401.
        HARTLEY, MARSDEN. "Tribute to Joyce Kilmer." *Poetry*, December, pp. 149–54.
1919   HARTLEY, MARSDEN. "Business of Poetry." *Poetry*, December, pp. 152–58.

1920   HARTLEY, MARSDEN. "Sunlight Persuasions." *Poetry*, May, pp. 59–70.

1921   ANDERSON GALLERIES, New York. *Seventy-Five Pictures by James N. Rosenberg and 117 Pictures by Marsden Hartley*. New York. (Catalogue for the auction sale held on May 21.)

 EGLINGTON, GUY C. "The Importance of Being 'Dada'." *International Studio*, November, p. lxiii.

HARTLEY, MARSDEN. *Adventures in the Arts*. New York.

HARTLEY, MARSDEN. "Crucifixion of Noël." *Dial*, April, pp. 378–80.

HARTLEY, MARSDEN. "Dissertation on Modern Painting." *Nation*, February 12, pp. 235–36.

ROSENFELD, PAUL. "American Painting." *Dial*, December, pp. 657–58.

SELIGMANN, HERBERT J. "The Elegance of Marsden Hartley." *International Studio*, October, pp. l–liii.

1923   DASBURG, ANDREW. "Cubism – Its Rise and Influence." *The Arts*, November, pp. 279–84.

HARTLEY, MARSDEN. "Greatest Show on Earth." *Vanity Fair*, August, pp. 33, 88.

HARTLEY, MARSDEN. *Twenty-Five Poems*. Paris.

1924   ROSENFELD, PAUL. *Port of New York*. New York. Pp. 83–101.

1925   ROSENFELD, PAUL. *Men Seen*. New York. Pp. 177–88.

1926   SOCIÉTÉ ANONYME. *International Exhibition*. Brooklyn.

1928   HARTLEY, MARSDEN. "Art – and the Personal Life." *Creative Art*, June, pp. xxxi–xxxvii.

1929   PEMBERTON, MURDOCK. "Soul Exposures." *Creative Art*, January, pp. xlvii–xlix.

1930   KOOTZ, SAMUEL M. *Modern American Painters*. New York. Pp. 40–42, plates 22–25.

1931   HARTLEY, MARSDEN. "New England on the Trapeze." *Creative Art*, February, supplement, pp. 57–58.

HARTLEY, MARSDEN. "The Paintings of Florine Stettheimer." *Creative Art*, July, pp. 18–23.

1932   DOWNTOWN GALLERY, New York. *Pictures of New England by a New Englander. Exhibition of Recent Paintings of Dogtown, Cape Ann, Massachusetts.* (Catalogue for the exhibition held from April 26 to May 15.)

"Hartley, Artist-Poet, Interprets New England." *Art Digest*, May 1, p. 15.

HARTLEY, MARSDEN. "Scenes: Bratigam: Window-Washer, Avenue C." *Poetry*, April, pp. 22–23.

McBRIDE, HENRY. "The Downtown Shows Marsden Hartley Paintings with a New England Touch." *New York Sun*, April 20.

1934   HARTLEY, MARSDEN. "291 – and the Brass Bowl," in *America and Alfred Stieglitz*. New York. Pp. 236–42; also, plate XV (C).

1935   WHITNEY MUSEUM OF AMERICAN ART, New York. *Abstract Painting in America*. New York.

1936   AN AMERICAN PLACE, New York. *Marsden Hartley's First Exhibition in Four Years*. (Catalogue of the exhibition held March 22 to April 14.)

DEVREE, HOWARD. "After Four Years." *New York Times*, March 29.

McBRIDE, HENRY. "Marsden Hartley Reappears." *New York Sun*, March 28.

McCAUSLAND, ELIZABETH. "Marsden Hartley Show at An American Place."

1936 *The Springfield* [Massachusetts] *Sunday Union and Republican*, April 12.
"Marsden Hartley — Painter." *Index of Twentieth Century Artists*, January, pp. 221+.
MUMFORD, LEWIS. "The Art Galleries." *New Yorker*, April 4, p. 58.

1937 AN AMERICAN PLACE. *Marsden Hartley: Exhibition of Recent Paintings, 1936.* (Catalogue for the exhibition held from April 20 to May 17.)
DAVIDSON, MARTHA. "Marsden Hartley: Paintings of the North." *Art News*, May 8, pp. 16–17.
HARTLEY, MARSDEN. "The Six Greatest New England Painters." *Yankee*, August, pp. 14–16.

1938 DAVIDSON, MARTHA. "The Climax of Hartley's Painting in Powerful Coastal Scenes." *Art News*, March 26, p. 21.
HUDSON WALKER GALLERY, New York. *Recent Paintings of Maine.* (Catalogue of the exhibition held from February 28 through April 2.)
McCAUSLAND, ELIZABETH. "Hartley at Walker Gallery." *Sunday Union and Republican*, March 6.
McCAUSLAND, ELIZABETH. Critical comment in a review of the Whitney Museum of American Art's annual exhibition of contemporary American painting. *Ibid.*, November 6.
"Not to 'Dilate over the Wrong Emotion'." *Art Digest*, March 15, p. 9.

1939 DOOLEY, WILLIAM GERMAIN. "Marsden Hartley." *Boston Evening Transcript*, December 23.
HUDSON WALKER GALLERY, New York. *Marsden Hartley.* (Catalogue of the exhibition held from March 6 to April 8.)
McCAUSLAND, ELIZABETH. "Marsden Hartley, Max Beckmann and Others." *Sunday Union and Republican*, March 5.
"Marsden Hartley Holds His 25th Solo Show." *Art Digest*, March 15, p. 52.
MUSICK, J. B. "Smelt Brook Falls." *Bulletin*, City Art Museum of St. Louis, April, pp. 21–22.

1939/1940 HARTLEY, MARSDEN. "Three Notes: Mary with the Child — of Leonardo, in the Pinakothek, Munich; Memling Portraits; Thinking of Gaston Lachaise." *Twice a Year*, Nos. 3–4, pp. 253–63.

1940 HARTLEY, MARSDEN. *Androscoggin*. Portland, Maine.
HUDSON WALKER GALLERY, New York. *Recent Paintings of Maine: Marsden Hartley.* (Catalogue of the exhibition held from March 11 to March 30.)
LANE, JAMES W. "The Virile Paintings of Marsden Hartley." *Art News*, March 16, p. 15.
McCAUSLAND, ELIZABETH. "Marsden Hartley Shows His Recent Paintings." *Sunday Union and Republican*, March 17.

1941 CINCINNATI MODERN ART SOCIETY, Cincinnati. *Marsden Hartley — Stuart Davis.* (Catalogue of the exhibition held from October 24 to November 24.)
HARTLEY, MARSDEN. Foreword, *Paintings and Drawings by John Blomshield.* New York. Pp. 3–5.
HARTLEY, MARSDEN. *Sea Burial*. Portland, Maine.
HARTLEY, MARSDEN. "Spring, 1941." *Story*, September–October, pp. 97–98.

1942 "Early Hartley Drawings on View." *Art Digest*, October 15, p. 11.

1942   HARTLEY, MARSDEN. "As to John Marin, and His Ideas," in *Water Colors, Oil Paintings, Etchings*. New York. Pp. 15–18.

KNOEDLER, M. & Co., New York. *Exhibition of Early Drawings by Marsden Hartley*. (Catalogue for the exhibition held from October 12 to October 31.)

MACBETH GALLERY, New York. *Marsden Hartley*. (Catalogue for the exhibition held from March 9 to March 28.)

"Marsden Hartley: He Seeks the Mystic Side of American Life." *Pictures on Exhibit*, March, pp. 10–11.

"Marsden Hartley in Successful Solo Show." *Art Digest*, March 15, p. 15.

MUSEUM OF MODERN ART, New York. *20th Century Portraits*. New York. Pp. 114–15, 137, 139.

ROSENBERG, PAUL, & Co., New York. *Recent Works by Marsden Hartley*. (Catalogue of the exhibition held from February 2 to February 27.)

1943   BOSWELL, HELEN. "Marsden Hartley Shows Rugged Paintings." *Art Digest*, February 15, p. 8.

"Marsden Hartley, Noted Artist, Dies." *New York Times*, September 3.

MELLQUIST, JEROME. "Marsden Hartley, Visionary Painter." *Commonweal*, December 31, pp. 276–78.

PHILLIPS MEMORIAL GALLERY, Washington, D.C. *Four Exhibitions . . . Paintings by Marsden Hartley*. (Catalogue of the exhibition held from October 24 to November 23.)

1944   ADAMS, PHILIP R. "Marsden Hartley Memorial." *Columbus Gallery of Fine Arts Bulletin*, January, pp. 1–2.

"Columbus Reviews Hartley." *Art Digest*, February 1, p. 21.

McCAUSLAND, ELIZABETH. "In Earned Recognition: Marsden Hartley's Work in Retrospective Show." *Sunday Union and Republican*, November 5.

MUSEUM OF MODERN ART, New York. *Lyonel Feininger: Marsden Hartley*. New York. Pp. [2–5], 53–96.

O'CONNOR, JOHN, JR. "New Paintings." *Carnegie Magazine*, January, pp. 245–48.

PHILLIPS, DUNCAN. "Marsden Hartley." *Magazine of Art*, March, pp. 82–87.

VALENTINER, W. R. "Log Jam, by Marsden Hartley." *Bulletin of the Detroit Institute of Arts*, January, p. 33.

1945   AN AMERICAN COLLECTION. *The Philadelphia Museum Bulletin*, May, pp. [74]–75. (Catalogue for the exhibition of the Alfred Stieglitz Collection at the Philadelphia Museum, before its dispersal to museums throughout the country. Many Hartleys were included.)

HARTLEY, MARSDEN. *Selected Poems*. Edited by Henry W. Wells. New York.

WATSON, E. W. "Two Painters: Roy Brown and Marsden Hartley." *American Artist*, May, pp. 12–18.

WELLS, HENRY W. "The Pictures and Poems of Marsden Hartley." *Magazine of Art*, January, pp. 26–30, 32.

1946   WHITNEY MUSEUM OF AMERICAN ART, New York. *Pioneers of Modern Art in America*. New York.

1947   WALKER, HUDSON D. "Marsden Hartley." *Kenyon Review*, Spring, pp. 248–59.

1948   COATES, ROBERT M. "Marsden Hartley's Maine." *New Yorker*, October 30, p. 85.

1948   GALLUP, DONALD C. "Weaving of a Pattern: Marsden Hartley and Gertrude Stein." *Magazine of Art*, November, pp. 256–61.
"The Work of Marsden Hartley." *Journal of the American Association of University Women*, Fall, pp. 6–8; also, cover and p. 5.

1950   *Journey into the Self: Being the Letters, Papers and Journals of Leo Stein.* Edited by Edmund Fuller. New York. P. 72.
YALE UNIVERSITY ART GALLERY. *Collection of the Société Anonyme: Museum of Modern Art 1920.* New Haven. Pp. 155–56.

1951   BAUR, JOHN I. H. *Revolution and Tradition in Modern American Art.* Cambridge, Massachusetts. Pp. 28, 39–40, 41, 43, 53, 54, 57, 69, 72, 73, 74, 133, 142; figures 36, 48, 66.
BROOKLYN MUSEUM, Brooklyn. *Revolution and Tradition: An Exhibition of the Chief Movements in American Painting from 1900 to the Present.* Brooklyn. Pp. 5, 6, 9, 11. (Catalog by John I. H. Baur.)
McCAUSLAND, ELIZABETH. *A. H. Maurer.* New York. Pp. 106, 112, 138, 151, 204.
MUSEUM OF MODERN ART, New York. *Abstract Painting and Sculpture in America.* New York. P. [55], 151.

(n.d.) HARTLEY, MARSDEN. "The Spangle of Existence." Unpublished.

(n.d.) UNIVERSITY OF MINNESOTA, THE UNIVERSITY GALLERY, Minneapolis. *5 Painters.* Minneapolis. Pp. 8–9. (Catalogue for an exhibition.)

36295

ND
237
H3435
M3

McCAUSLAND, ELIZABETH
MARSDEN HARTLEY.

DATE DUE

Fernald Library
Colby-Sawyer College
New London, New Hampshire

GAYLORD   PRINTED IN U.S.A.

WELLS BINDERY

APR   1982

WALTHAM, MA 02154